Welcome to *Interchange Fourth Edition*, the world's most successful English series!

Interchange offers a complete set of tools for learning how to communicate in English.

Student's Book

with NEW Self-study DVD-ROM

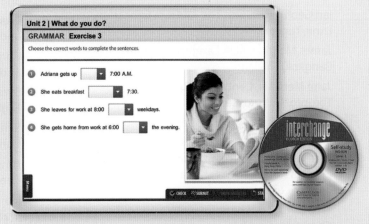

- **Complete video program** with additional **video exercises**

- Additional **vocabulary, grammar, speaking, listening,** and **reading** practice
- Printable **score reports** to submit to teachers

Available online

Interchange Arcade

- **Free** self-study website
- **Fun**, interactive, self-scoring activities
- Practice **vocabulary, grammar, listening,** and **reading**
- **MP3s** of the class audio program

Online Workbook

- A variety of **interactive activities** that correspond to each Student's Book lesson
- **Instant feedback** for hundreds of activities
- **Easy to use** with clear, easy-to-follow instructions
- Extra **listening practice**
- Simple tools for teachers to **monitor progress** such as scores, attendance, and time spent online

Authors' acknowledgments

A great number of people contributed to the development of *Interchange Fourth Edition*. Particular thanks are owed to the reviewers using *Interchange*, *Third Edition* in the following schools and institutes – their insights and suggestions have helped define the content and format of the fourth edition:

Ian Geoffrey Hanley, **The Address Education Center**, Izmir, Turkey

James McBride, **AUA Language Center**, Bangkok, Thailand

Jane Merivale, **Centennial College**, Toronto, Ontario, Canada

Elva Elena Peña Andrade, **Centro de Auto Aprendizaje de Idiomas**, Nuevo León, Mexico

José Paredes, **Centro de Educación Continua de la Escuela Politécnica Nacional** (CEC-EPN), Quito, Ecuador

Chia-jung Tsai, **Changhua University of Education**, Changhua City, Taiwan

Kevin Liang, **Chinese Culture University**, Taipei, Taiwan

Roger Alberto Neira Perez, **Colegio Santo Tomás de Aquino**, Bogotá, Colombia

Teachers at **Escuela Miguel F. Martínez**, Monterrey, Mexico

Maria Virgínia Goulart Borges de Lebron, **Great Idiomas**, São Paulo, Brazil

Gina Kim, **Hoseo University**, Chungnam, South Korea

Heeyong Kim, Seoul, South Korea

Elisa Borges, **IBEU-Rio**, Rio de Janeiro, Brazil

Jason M. Ham, **Inha University**, Incheon, South Korea

Rita de Cássia S. Silva Miranda, **Instituto Batista de Idiomas**, Belo Horizonte, Brazil

Teachers at **Instituto Politécnico Nacional**, Mexico City, Mexico

Victoria M. Roberts and Regina Marie Williams, **Interactive College of Technology**, Chamblee, Georgia, USA

Teachers at **Internacional de Idiomas**, Mexico City, Mexico

Marcelo Serafim Godinho, **Life Idiomas**, São Paulo, Brazil

J. Kevin Varden, **Meiji Gakuin University**, Yokohama, Japan

Rosa Maria Valencia Rodríguez, Mexico City, Mexico

Chung-Ju Fan, **National Kinmen Institute of Technology**, Kinmen, Taiwan

Shawn Beasom, **Nihon Daigaku**, Tokyo, Japan

Gregory Hadley, **Niigata University of International and Information Studies**, Niigata, Japan

Chris Ruddenklau, **Osaka University of Economics and Law**, Osaka, Japan

Byron Roberts, **Our Lady of Providence Girls' High School**, Xindian City, Taiwan

Simon Banha, **Phil Young's English School**, Curitiba, Brazil

Flávia Gonçalves Carneiro Braathen, **Real English Center**, Viçosa, Brazil

Márcia Cristina Barboza de Miranda, **SENAC**, Recife, Brazil

Raymond Stone, **Seneca College of Applied Arts and Technology**, Toronto, Ontario, Canada

Gen Murai, **Takushoku University**, Tokyo, Japan

Teachers at **Tecnológico de Estudios Superiores de Ecatepec**, Mexico City, Mexico

Teachers at **Universidad Autónoma Metropolitana–Azcapotzalco**, Mexico City, Mexico

Teachers at **Universidad Autónoma de Nuevo León**, Monterrey, Mexico

Mary Grace Killian Reyes, **Universidad Autónoma de Tamaulipas**, Tampico Tamaulipas, Mexico

Teachers at **Universidad Estatal del Valle de Ecatepec**, Mexico City, Mexico

Teachers at **Universidad Nacional Autónoma de Mexico – Zaragoza**, Mexico City, Mexico

Teachers at **Universidad Nacional Autónoma de Mexico – Iztacala**, Mexico City, Mexico

Luz Edith Herrera Diaz, Veracruz, Mexico

Seri Park, **YBM PLS**, Seoul, South Korea

Self-assessment charts revised by Alex Tilbury

Grammar plus written by Karen Davy

interchange
FOURTH EDITION

Jack C. Richards
With Jonathan Hull and Susan Proctor

Series Editor: David Bohlke

CAMBRIDGE
UNIVERSITY PRESS

STUDENT'S BOOK 1A

CAMBRIDGE UNIVERSITY PRESS
Cambridge, New York, Melbourne, Madrid, Cape Town,
Singapore, São Paulo, Delhi, Mexico City

Cambridge University Press
32 Avenue of the Americas, New York, NY 10013-2473, USA

www.cambridge.org
Information on this title: www.cambridge.org/9781107694439

First published 1997
Third edition 2005
3rd printing 2013

Printed in Hong Kong, China, by Golden Cup Printing Company Limited

A catalog record for this publication is available from the British Library.

ISBN 978-1-107-64867-8 Student's Book 1 with Self-study DVD-ROM
ISBN 978-1-107-69443-9 Student's Book 1A with Self-study DVD-ROM
ISBN 978-1-107-67396-0 Student's Book 1B with Self-study DVD-ROM
ISBN 978-1-107-64872-2 Workbook 1
ISBN 978-1-107-61687-5 Workbook 1A
ISBN 978-1-107-69959-5 Workbook 1B
ISBN 978-1-107-69917-5 Teacher's Edition 1 with Assessment Audio CD/CD-ROM
ISBN 978-1-107-64725-1 Class Audio 1 CDs
ISBN 978-1-107-67993-1 Full Contact 1with Self-study DVD-ROM
ISBN 978-1-107-61136-8 Full Contact 1A with Self-study DVD-ROM
ISBN 978-1-107-63780-1 Full Contact 1B with Self-study DVD-ROM

For a full list of components, visit www.cambridge.org/interchange

Art direction, book design, layout services, and photo research: Integra
Audio production: CityVox, NYC
Video production: Nesson Media Boston, Inc.

Plan of Book 1A

1 Please call me Beth.

1 CONVERSATION *Where are you from?*

▶ Listen and practice.

David: Hello, I'm David Garza. I'm a new club member.

Beth: Hi. My name is Elizabeth Silva, but please call me Beth.

David: OK. Where are you from, Beth?

Beth: Brazil. How about you?

David: I'm from Mexico.

Beth: Oh, I love Mexico! It's really beautiful.

Beth: Oh, good. Sun-hee is here.

David: Who's Sun-hee?

Beth: She's my classmate. We're in the same math class.

David: Where's she from?

Beth: South Korea. Let's go and say hello. Sorry, what's your last name again? Garcia?

David: Actually, it's Garza.

Beth: How do you spell that?

David: G-A-R-Z-A.

2 SPEAKING *Checking information*

A ▶ Match the questions with the responses. Listen and check. Then practice with a partner. Give your own information.

1. I'm sorry. What's your name again? ....
2. What do people call you? ....
3. How do you spell your last name? ....

a. S-I-L-V-A.
b. It's Elizabeth Silva.
c. Everyone calls me Beth.

B GROUP WORK Introduce yourself with your full name. Use the expressions in part A. Make a list of names for your group.

A: Hi! I'm Yuriko Noguchi.
B: I'm sorry. What's your last name again? . . .

3 CONVERSATION *What's Seoul like?*

A ▶ Listen and practice.

Beth: Sun-hee, this is David Garza. He's a
 new club member from Mexico.
Sun-hee: Nice to meet you, David. I'm
 Sun-hee Park.
David: Hi. So, you're from South Korea?
Sun-hee: That's right. I'm from Seoul.
David: That's cool. What's Seoul like?
Sun-hee: It's really nice. It's a very
 exciting city.

B ▶ Listen to the rest of the conversation.
What city is David from? What's it like?

4 PRONUNCIATION *Linked sounds*

▶ Listen and practice. Notice how final consonant sounds are often linked to
the vowels that follow them.

I'm a new club member.   Sun-hee is over there.   My name is Elizabeth Silva.

5 GRAMMAR FOCUS

Statements with be; possessive adjectives ▶

Statements with **be**	Contractions of **be**	Possessive adjectives
I**'m** from Mexico.	I**'m** = I am	my
You**'re** from Brazil.	you**'re** = you are	your
He**'s** from Japan.	he**'s** = he is	his
She**'s** a new club member.	she**'s** = she is	her
It**'s** an exciting city.	it**'s** = it is	its
We**'re** in the same class.	we**'re** = we are	our
They**'re** my classmates.	they**'re** = they are	their

A Complete these sentences. Then tell a partner about yourself.

1. ...My... name is Mariko Kimura. .... from Japan. .... family is in Osaka.
.... brother is a university student. .... name is Kenji.

2. .... name is Antonio. .... from Buenos Aires. .... a really nice city. .... sister
is a student here, too. .... parents are in Argentina right now.

3. .... Katherine, but everyone calls me Katie. .... last name is Martin. .... a
student at City College. .... parents are on vacation this week. .... in Los Angeles.

> ## Wh-questions with be ▶
>
> | | |
> |---|---|
> | **Where's** your friend? | He's in class. |
> | **Who's** Sun-hee? | She's my classmate. |
> | **What's** Seoul **like**? | It's a very exciting city. |
> | | |
> | **Where are** you and Luisa from? | We're from Brazil. |
> | **How are** your classes? | They're pretty interesting. |
> | **What are** your classmates **like**? | They're really nice. |

B Complete these questions. Then practice with a partner.

1. A: ...._Who's_......... that?
   B: Oh, that's Miss West.

2. A: .... she from?
   B: She's from Miami.

3. A: .... her first name?
   B: It's Celia.

4. A: .... the two students over there?
   B: Their names are Jeremy and Karen.

5. A: .... they from?
   B: They're from Vancouver, Canada.

6. A: .... they .... ?
   B: They're shy, but very friendly.

C **GROUP WORK** Write five questions about your classmates.
Then ask and answer the questions.

> What's your last name?
> Where's Ming from?

6 SNAPSHOT

GREETINGS *from around the world*

a handshake — the United States

a kiss on the cheek

a bow

a hug

a pat on the back

a fist bump

Sources: www.familyeducation.com; www.time.com

Which greetings are typical in your country?
Can you write the name of a country for each greeting?
What are other ways to greet people?

7 CONVERSATION *How's it going?*

▶ Listen and practice.

Sun-hee: Hey, David. How's it going?
David: Fine, thanks. How are you?
Sun-hee: Pretty good. So, are your classes
interesting this semester?
David: Yes, they are. I really love chemistry.
Sun-hee: Chemistry? Are you and Beth in the
same class?
David: No, we aren't. My class is in the
morning. Her class is in the afternoon.
Sun-hee: Listen, I'm on my way to the cafeteria
now. Are you free?
David: Sure. Let's go.

8 GRAMMAR FOCUS

Yes/No questions and short answers with be ▶

Are you free?	Yes, I **am**.	No, I**'m not**.
Is David from Mexico?	Yes, he **is**.	No, he**'s not**./No, he **isn't**.
Is Beth's class in the morning?	Yes, it **is**.	No, it**'s not**./No, it **isn't**.
Are you and Beth in the same class?	Yes, we **are**.	No, we**'re not**./No, we **aren't**.
Are your classes interesting?	Yes, they **are**.	No, they**'re not**./No, they **aren't**.

A Complete these conversations. Then practice with a partner.

1. A: ....Is.... Ms. Gray from the United States?
   B: Yes, she .... from Chicago.

2. A: .... English class at 10:00?
   B: No, it .... at 11:00.

3. A: .... you and Monique from France?
   B: Yes, we .... from Paris.

4. A: .... Mr. and Mrs. Tavares American?
   B: No, they .... Brazilian.

B Answer these questions. If you answer "no," give the correct
information. Then ask your partner the questions.

1. Are you from the United States? ....
2. Is your teacher from Canada? ....
3. Is your English class in the morning? ....
4. Are you and your best friend the same age? ....

C **GROUP WORK** Write five questions about your classmates.
Then ask and answer the questions.

> Are Cindy and Brian from Los Angeles?

9 WORD POWER *Hello and good-bye*

A Do you know these expressions? Which ones are "hellos" and which ones are "good-byes"? Complete the chart. Add expressions of your own.

✓ Bye.
✓ Good morning.
  Good night.
  Have a good day.
  Hey.
  Hi.

How are you?
How's it going?
See you later.
See you tomorrow.
Talk to you later.
What's up?

Hello	Good-bye
Good morning.	Bye.

B Match each expression with the best response.

1. Have a good day.
2. Hi. How are you?
3. What's up?
4. Good morning.

a. Oh, not much.
b. Thank you. You, too.
c. Good morning.
d. Pretty good, thanks.

C CLASS ACTIVITY Practice saying hello. Then practice saying good-bye.

A: Hi, Aki. How's it going?
B: Pretty good, thanks. How are you?

10 LISTENING *What's your last name again?*

Listen to the conversations. Complete the information about each person.

	First name	Last name	Where from?
1.	Chris		
2.		Sanchez	
3.	Min-ho		

11 INTERCHANGE 1 *Getting to know you*

Find out about your classmates. Go to Interchange 1 on page 114.

What's in a Name?

Look at the names in the article. Do you know any people with these names? What are they like?

Your name is very important. When you think of yourself, you probably think of your name first. It is an important part of your identity.

Right now, the two most popular names for babies in the United States are "Jacob" for boys and "Emma" for girls. Why are these names popular? And why are other names unpopular?

Names can become popular because of famous actors, TV or book characters, or athletes. Popular names suggest very positive things. Unpopular names suggest negative things. Surprisingly, people generally agree on the way they feel about names. Here are some common opinions about names from a recent survey.

HELLO
my name is
_____

Boys' names
George: average, boring
Jacob: creative, friendly
Michael: good-looking, athletic
Stanley: nerdy, serious

Girls' names
Betty: old-fashioned, average
Emma: independent, adventurous
Jane: plain, ordinary
Nicole: beautiful, intelligent

So why do parents give their children unpopular names? One reason is tradition. Many people are named after a family member. Of course, opinions can change over time. A name that is unpopular now may become popular in the future. That's good news for all the Georges and Bettys out there!

A Read the article. Then check (✓) the statements that are true.

1. Your name is part of your identity.
2. People often feel the same way about a particular name.
3. Boys' names are more popular than girls' names.
4. People are often named after family members.
5. Opinions about names can change.

B According to the article, which names suggest positive things? Which suggest negative things? Complete the chart.

Positive names		Negative names	

C PAIR WORK What names are popular in your country? Why are they popular?

2 What do you do?

1 SNAPSHOT

Top Six Student Part-Time Jobs in the United States

1 usher
2 tutor
3 team assistant
4 caregiver
5 server
6 fitness instructor

Source: www.snagajob.com

Which jobs are easy? Which are difficult? Why?
What's your opinion? Are these good jobs for students?
What are some other student jobs?

2 WORD POWER

A Complete the word map with jobs from the list.

- ✓ accountant
- ✓ cashier
-   chef
- ✓ dancer
- ✓ flight attendant
-   musician
-   pilot
-   receptionist
-   server
-   singer
-   tour guide
-   website designer

Office work
accountant

Food service
cashier

Jobs

Travel industry
flight attendant

Entertainment business
dancer

B Add two more jobs to each category. Then compare with a partner.

3 SPEAKING Work and workplaces

A Look at the pictures. Match the information in columns A, B, and C.

A	B	C
a salesperson	builds houses	in a restaurant
a chef	cares for patients	for a construction company
a mechanic	writes stories	in a hospital
a carpenter	cooks food	in a garage
a reporter	fixes cars	in a department store
a nurse	sells clothes	for a newspaper

B **PAIR WORK** Take turns describing each person's job.

A: She's a salesperson. She sells clothes. She works in a department store.
B: And he's a chef. He . . .

4 CONVERSATION Where do you work?

A ▶ Listen and practice.

Jason: Where do you work, Andrea?
Andrea: I work at Thomas Cook Travel.
Jason: Oh, really? What do you do there?
Andrea: I'm a guide. I take people on tours to countries in South America, like Peru.
Jason: How interesting!
Andrea: Yeah, it's a great job. I really love it. And what do you do?
Jason: Oh, I'm a student. I have a part-time job, too.
Andrea: Where do you work?
Jason: In a fast-food restaurant.
Andrea: Which restaurant?
Jason: Hamburger Heaven.

B ▶ Listen to the rest of the conversation. What does Jason do, exactly? How does he like his job?

Simple present Wh-questions and statements ▶

What do you **do**?	I**'m** a student. I **have** a part-time job, too.	**I/You**	**He/She**
Where do you **work**?	I **work** at Hamburger Heaven.	work	works
Where do you **go** to school?	I **go** to the University of Texas.	take	takes
		study	studies
What does Andrea **do**?	She's a guide. She **takes** people on tours.	teach	teaches
Where does she **work**?	She **works** at Thomas Cook Travel.	do	does
How does she **like** it?	She **loves** it.	go	goes
		have	has

A Complete these conversations. Then practice with a partner.

1. A: What ......*do*...... you ......*do*...... ?
    B: I'm a full-time student. I study the violin.
    A: And .... do you .... to school?
    B: I .... to the New York School of Music.
    A: Wow! .... do you like your classes?
    B: I .... them a lot.

2. A: What .... Tanya do?
    B: She's a teacher. She .... an art class
       at a school in Denver.
    A: And what about Ryan? Where .... he work?
    B: He .... for a big computer company in
       San Francisco.
    A: .... does he do, exactly?
    B: He's a website designer. He .... fantastic
       websites.

B **PAIR WORK** What do you know about these jobs?
Complete the chart. Then write sentences about each job.

A reporter	A flight attendant	A teacher
works for a newspaper	....	....
interviews people	....	....
writes stories	....	....

A reporter works for a newspaper, interviews people, and writes stories.

C **PAIR WORK** Ask your partner questions like these about work
and school. Take notes to use in Exercise 6.

What do you do?	Do you go to school?	How do you like . . . ?
Where do you live?	Do you have a job?	What's your favorite . . . ?

6 WRITING *A biography*

A Use your notes from Exercise 5 to write a biography of your partner. Don't use your partner's name. Use *he* or *she* instead.

> My partner is a student. She lives near the university. She studies fashion design at the Fashion Institute. Her favorite class is History of Design. She has a part-time job in a clothing store. She loves her job and . . .

B CLASS ACTIVITY Pass your biographies around the class. Guess who each biography is about.

7 CONVERSATION *I start work at five.*

A ⏵ Listen and practice.

Kevin: So, do you usually come to the gym in the morning?
Allie: Yeah, I do. I usually come here at 10:00.
Kevin: Really? What time do you go to work?
Allie: Oh, I work in the afternoon. I start work at five.
Kevin: Wow, that's late. When do you get home at night?
Allie: I usually get home at midnight.
Kevin: Midnight? That *is* late. What do you do, exactly?
Allie: I'm a chef. I work at the Pink Elephant.
Kevin: That's my favorite restaurant! By the way, I'm Kevin. . . .

B ⏵ Listen to the rest of the conversation. What time does Kevin get up? start work?

8 PRONUNCIATION *Syllable stress*

A ⏵ Listen and practice. Notice which syllable has the main stress.

⬤ ○	⬤ ○ ○	○ ⬤ ○
dancer	salesperson	accountant
....	....	....
....	....	....

B ⏵ Which stress pattern do these words have? Add them to the columns in part A. Then listen and check.

carpenter   caregiver   musician   reporter   server   tutor

9 GRAMMAR FOCUS

Time expressions ▶

				Expressing clock time
I get up	**at** 6:00	**in** the morning	**on** weekdays.	6:00
I go to bed	**around** ten	**in** the evening	**on** weeknights.	six
I leave work	**early**	**in** the afternoon	**on** weekends.	six o'clock
I get home	**late**	**at** night	**on** Fridays.	6:00 A.M. = 6:00 in the morning
I stay up	**until** midnight	**on** Saturdays.		6:00 P.M. = 6:00 in the evening
I exercise	**before** noon	**on** Saturdays.		
I wake up	**after** noon	**on** Sundays.		

A Circle the correct words.

1. I get up (at)/ until six at / on weekdays.
2. I have lunch at / early 11:30 in / on Mondays.
3. I have a little snack in / around 10:00 in / at night.
4. In / On Fridays, I leave school early / before.
5. I stay up before / until 1:00 A.M. in / on weekends.
6. I sleep until / around noon in / on Sundays.

B Rewrite the sentences in part A so that they are true for you. Then compare with a partner.

C PAIR WORK Take turns asking and answering these questions.

1. Which days do you get up early? late?
2. What's something you do before 8:00 in the morning?
3. What's something you do on Saturday evenings?
4. What do you do only on Sundays?

10 LISTENING Daily schedules

A ▶ Listen to Greg, Megan, and Lori talk about their daily schedules. Complete the chart.

	Job	Gets up at . . .	Gets home at . . .	Goes to bed at . . .
Greg	mechanic			
Megan		7:00 a.m.		
Lori				

B CLASS ACTIVITY Who do you think has the best daily schedule? Why?

11 INTERCHANGE 2 Common ground

Find out about your classmates' schedules. Go to Interchange 2 on page 115.

Why do you need a job?

Scan the profiles. Who is in high school? Who is in college? Who is a new parent?

These people need jobs. Read about their schedules, experience, and why they need a job.

Julia Brown

I study French and want to be a teacher someday. I have classes all day on Monday, Tuesday, and Thursday, and on Wednesday and Friday afternoons. I usually study on weekends. I need a job because college is really expensive! I don't have any experience, but I'm a fast learner.

Eddie Chen

I'm 16 now, and my parents don't give me an allowance anymore. I want to earn some money because I like to go out with my friends on the weekend. I go to school at 8:00 and get home around 4:30. My parents own a restaurant, so I know a little about restaurant work.

Denise Parker

My husband is an accountant and makes good money, but we don't save very much. We live in a small apartment, and we have a new baby. We want to save money to buy a house. I take care of the baby, so I need a job I can do at home. I can type well, and I have a new computer.

A Read the article. Why do these people need jobs? Check (✓) the correct boxes.

	Julia	Denise	Eddie
1. To save money	☐	☐	☐
2. To pay for college	☐	☐	☐
3. To go out on the weekend	☐	☐	☐
4. To buy a house	☐	☐	☐

B **PAIR WORK** Choose the best job for each person. Explain why.

Chef	**English Tutor**	**Caregiver**
French and Italian cooking	*Flexible work hours*	*Work with children*
Weekends only	*$10 an hour*	*Earn great money*
Server	**Receptionist**	**Online Salesperson**
Evenings only	*Mornings and afternoons*	*Work at home*
Experience a plus	*No experience necessary*	*Earn up to $20 an hour*

Units 1–2 Progress check

SELF-ASSESSMENT

How well can you do these things? Check (✓) the boxes.

I can	Very well	OK	A little
Make an introduction and use basic greeting expressions (Ex. 1)	☐	☐	☐
Show I didn't understand and ask for repetition (Ex. 1)	☐	☐	☐
Ask and answer questions about myself and other people (Ex. 2)	☐	☐	☐
Ask and answer questions about work (Ex. 3, 4)	☐	☐	☐
Ask and answer questions about habits and routines (Ex. 5)	☐	☐	☐

 ROLE PLAY *Introductions*

A **PAIR WORK** You are talking to someone at school. Have a conversation.

A: Hi. How are you?
B: . . .
A: By the way, my name is . . .
B: I'm sorry. What's your name again?
A: . . .
B: I'm . . . . Are you a student here?
A: . . . And how about you?
B: . . .
A: Oh, really? And where are you from?

B **GROUP WORK** Join another pair.
Introduce your partner.

 SPEAKING *Interview*

Write questions for these answers. Then use the questions to interview a classmate.

1. What's .... ?	My name is Keiko Kawakami.
2. .... ?	I'm from Osaka, Japan.
3. .... ?	Yes, my classes are very interesting.
4. .... ?	My favorite class is English.
5. .... ?	No, my teacher isn't American.
6. .... ?	My classmates are very nice.
7. .... ?	My best friend is Maria.

3 SPEAKING *What a job!*

A What do you know about these jobs? List three things each person does.

receptionist

tour guide

cashier

teacher

takes messages ....

B GROUP WORK Compare your lists. Take turns asking about the jobs.

4 LISTENING *Work and school*

A Listen to James and Lindsey talk at a party. Complete the chart.

	James	Lindsey
What do you do?	....	....
Where do you work/study?	....	....
How do you like your job/classes?	....	....
What do you do after work/school?	....	....

B PAIR WORK Practice the questions in part A. Answer with your own information.

5 SURVEY *My perfect day*

A Imagine your perfect day. Complete the chart with your own answers.

What time do you get up?	....
What do you do after you get up?	....
Where do you go?	....
What do you do in the evening?	....
When do you go to bed?	....

B PAIR WORK Talk about your perfect day. Answer any questions.

WHAT'S NEXT?

Look at your Self-assessment again. Do you need to review anything?

3 How much is it?

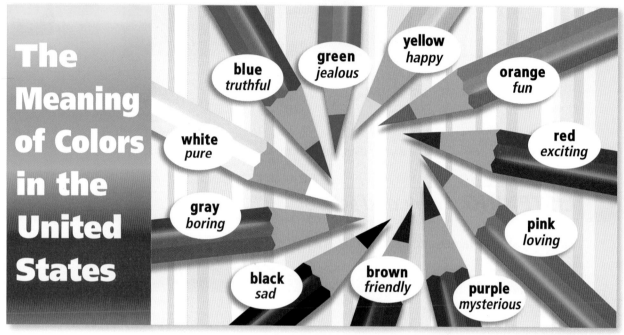

The Meaning of Colors in the United States

blue
truthful

green
jealous

yellow
happy

orange
fun

white
pure

red
exciting

gray
boring

pink
loving

black
sad

brown
friendly

purple
mysterious

Sources: Based on information from Think Quest; Hewlett-Packard, *The Meaning of Color*

Which words have a positive meaning? Which have a negative meaning?
What meanings do these colors have for you?
What does your favorite color make you think of?

2 CONVERSATION *It's really pretty.*

A ▶ Listen and practice.

Salesclerk: Can I help you?
Customer: Yes, thank you. How much are these gloves?
Salesclerk: The gray ones? They're $18.
Customer: Oh, that's not bad. Do they come in black?
Salesclerk: No, sorry, just gray.
Customer: OK. Um, how much is that scarf?
Salesclerk: Which one? The blue and orange one?
Customer: No, the yellow one.
Salesclerk: Let's see . . . it's $24.95.
Customer: It's really pretty. I'll take it.

B ▶ Listen to the rest of the conversation. What else does the customer look at? Does she buy it?

Demonstratives; one, ones ▶

79¢	= seventy-nine cents
$18	= eighteen dollars
$24.95	= twenty-four ninety-five

How much is	**this** scarf?	**that** scarf?	Which **one**?	**It's** $24.95.
	this one?	**that one**?	The yellow **one**.	
How much are	**these** gloves?	**those** gloves?	Which **ones**?	**They're** $18.
	these?	**those**?	The gray **ones**.	

A Complete these conversations. Then practice with a partner.

1

A: Excuse me. How much
   are ....*those*.... jeans?
B: Which .... ? Do you
   mean .... ?
A: No, the light blue ....
B: Oh, ... are $59.95.
A: Wow! That's expensive!

2

A: How much is .... backpack?
B: Which .... ?
A: The red ....
B: It's $36.99. But ....
   green .... is only $22.25.
A: That's not bad. Can I see it, please?

B **PAIR WORK** Add prices to the items. Then ask and answer questions.

A: How much are these sunglasses?
B: Which ones?
A: The pink ones.
B: They're $86.99.
A: That's expensive!

useful expressions

That's cheap.
That's reasonable.
That's OK/not bad.
That's expensive.

4 PRONUNCIATION *Sentence stress*

A ▶ Listen and practice. Notice that the important words in a sentence have more stress.

Excuse me.   That's expensive.   I'll take it.   Do you mean these?

B PAIR WORK Practice the conversations in Exercise 3, part B again. Pay attention to the sentence stress.

5 ROLE PLAY *Can I help you?*

A PAIR WORK Put items "for sale" on your desk, such as notebooks, watches, phones, or bags.

Student A: You are a salesclerk. Answer the customer's questions.
Student B: You are a customer. Ask the price of each item. Say if you want to buy it.

A: Can I help you?
B: Yes. I like these sunglasses. How much are they?
A: Which ones?

B Change roles and try the role play again.

6 LISTENING *Look at this!*

A ▶ Listen to two friends shopping. Write the color and price for each item.

Item	Color	Price	Do they buy it?	
			Yes	**No**
1. phone	....	....	☐	☐
2. watch	....	....	☐	☐
3. sunglasses	....	....	☐	☐
4. T-shirt	....	....	☐	☐

B ▶ Listen again. Do they buy the items? Check (✓) Yes or No.

7 INTERCHANGE 3 *Flea market*

See what kinds of deals you can make as a buyer and a seller.
Go to Interchange 3 on pages 116–117.

WORD POWER *Materials*

A What are these things made of? Label each one. Use the words from the list.

cotton	gold	leather	plastic
rubber	silk	silver	wool

1. a ......*silk*...... tie

2. a .... bracelet

3. a .... ring

4. a .... shirt

5. a .... jacket

6. .... earrings

7. .... boots

8. .... socks

B **PAIR WORK** What other materials are the things in part A sometimes made of? Make a list.

C **CLASS ACTIVITY** Which materials can you find in your classroom?

"Pedro has a cotton shirt, and Ellen has leather shoes."

CONVERSATION *I prefer the blue one.*

A ▶ Listen and practice.

Brett: These wool sweaters are really nice. Which one do you like better?

Lisa: Let's see . . . I like the green one more.

Brett: The green one? Why?

Lisa: It looks warmer.

Brett: That's true, but I think I prefer the blue one. It's more stylish than the green one.

Lisa: Hmm. There's no price tag.

Brett: Excuse me. How much is this sweater?

Clerk: It's $139. Would you like to try it on?

Brett: Uh, no. That's OK. But thanks anyway.

Clerk: You're welcome.

B ▶ Listen to the rest of the conversation. What does Brett buy? What does Lisa think of it?

10 GRAMMAR FOCUS

Preferences; comparisons with adjectives ▶

Which sweater do you **prefer**?
   I **prefer** the blue one.
Which one do you **like more**?
   I **like** the blue one **more**.
Which one do you **like better**?
   I **like** the blue one **better**.

It's **nicer than** the green one.

It's **prettier than** the green one.

It's **more stylish than** the green one.

Spelling

cheap ⟶ cheaper
nice ⟶ nicer
pretty ⟶ prettier
big ⟶ bigger

A Complete these conversations. Then practice with a partner.

1. A: Which of these jackets do you like more?
   B: I prefer the leather one. The design is .... (nice), and it looks .... (expensive) the wool one.

2. A: These T-shirts are nice. Which one do you prefer?
   B: I like the green and white one better. The colors are .... (pretty). It's .... (attractive) the gray and black one.

3. A: Which earrings do you like better?
   B: I like the silver ones more. They're .... (big) the gold ones. And they're .... (cheap).

B **PAIR WORK** Compare the things in part A. Give your own opinions.

A: Which jacket do you like more?
B: I like the wool one better. The color is prettier.

useful expressions

The color is prettier.
The design is nicer.
The style is more attractive.
The material is better.

11 WRITING *Comparing prices*

How much do these things cost in your country? Complete the chart.
Then compare the prices in your country with the prices in the U.S.

	Price in my country	Price in the U.S.
a cup of coffee	....	$1.40
a movie ticket	....	$12.50
a paperback novel	....	$8.95
a video game	....	$50.00

Many things are more expensive in my country than in the United States. For example, a cup of coffee costs about $2.00 at home. In the U.S., it's cheaper. It's only $1.40. A movie ticket costs . . .

12 READING

Tools for Better Shopping

Scan the article. Find the names of popular websites. Do you use any of them for shopping?

1 Do you like to shop online? Like millions of people, you want to find the best things for the best price. There are so many choices that it can be difficult to find the things you need and want. Here's where technology comes in! Popular websites like Facebook and Twitter aren't just for social networking anymore.

2 The websites Facebook and Twitter are popular because people can connect to friends and get their most recent news. But people also use these sites as powerful shopping tools. Members can ask about an item and then get opinions from people they trust. Twitterers can also search for news from other users and then find stores nearby that sell the item.

3 Another helpful shopping tool is the smartphone. Smartphone users can go into a store, find an item they like, and then type the item number into their smartphone. They can compare prices, read reviews, and make better decisions about their purchase. Many people find a better price online or at another store. People often want to see and touch an item before they buy. They can do just that – and pay a lower price, too.

4 But you don't have to be a Facebook or Twitter member or have a smartphone to find a bargain. Websites like Shopzilla compare prices, give reviews, and find stores near you with the best bargains. Google does all these things but also lets you buy items directly through its site. Be a smart shopper. The information you need is at your fingertips!

A Read the article. Answer these questions. Then write the number of the paragraph where you find each answer.

.... a. How are Shopzilla and Google similar? ....

.... b. What are Twitter users called? ....

.... c. How do smartphones help find bargains? ....

.... d. What are two social networking sites? ....

B According to the article, which shopping tools do these things? Check (✓) the correct boxes.

	Facebook	Twitter	Smartphone	Shopzilla	Google
1. get opinions from friends	☐	☐	☐	☐	☐
2. find product reviews	☐	☐	☐	☐	☐
3. compare prices	☐	☐	☐	☐	☐
4. find stores with items you want	☐	☐	☐	☐	☐
5. buy items directly	☐	☐	☐	☐	☐

C **PAIR WORK** Do you shop mostly in stores or online? How do you find good prices?

4 I really like hip-hop.

Music Sales in the United States

Rock	Other	Classical	Jazz	Gospel	Hip-hop	R&B	Pop	Country	New Age
32%	15%	2%	1%	7%	11%	10%	9%	12%	1%

Source: The Recording Industry Association of America, *2008 Consumer Profile*

▶ Listen and number the musical styles from 1 to 9.
Which of these styles of music are popular in your country?
What other kinds of music are popular in your country?

2 WORD POWER

A Complete the word map with words from the list.

action   reality show
electronic   reggae
game show   salsa
heavy metal   science fiction
horror   soap opera
musical   talk show

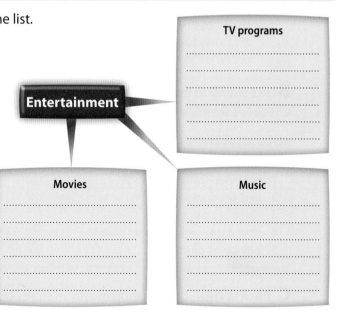

TV programs

Entertainment

Movies

Music

B Add two more words to each category.
Then compare with a partner.

C GROUP WORK Number the items
in each list from 1 (you like it the most)
to 6 (you like it the least). Then compare
your ideas.

3 CONVERSATION *Who's your favorite singer?*

A ◉ Listen and practice.

Marissa: Do you like country music, Brian?

Brian: No, I don't like it very much. Do you?

Marissa: Yeah, I do. I'm a big fan of Taylor Swift.

Brian: I think I know her. Does she play the guitar?

Marissa: Yes, she does. She's a really good musician. So, what kind of music do you like?

Brian: I really like hip-hop.

Marissa: Oh, yeah? Who's your favorite singer?

Brian: Jay-Z. Do you like him?

Marissa: No, I don't. I don't like hip-hop very much.

B ◉ Listen to the rest of the conversation. Who is Brian's favorite group? Does Marissa like them?

4 GRAMMAR FOCUS

Simple present questions; short answers ◉

		Object pronouns
Do you **like** country music? Yes, I **do**. I love it. No, I **don't**. I don't like it very much.	**What kind of** music **do** you **like**? I really like hip-hop.	me you him
Does she **play** the piano? Yes, she **does**. She plays very well. No, she **doesn't**. She doesn't play an instrument.	**What does** she **play**? She plays the guitar.	her it us
Do they **like** Green Day? Yes, they **do**. They like them a lot. No, they **don't**. They don't like them at all.	**Who do** they **like**? They like Coldplay.	them

Complete these conversations. Then practice with a partner.

1. A: I like Kings of Leon a lot. .... you know .... ?
   B: Yes, I .... , and I love this song. Let's download ....
2. A: .... you like science fiction movies?
   B: Yes, I .... I like .... very much.
3. A: .... Kevin and Emma like soap operas?
   B: Kevin .... , but Emma .... She hates ....
4. A: What kind of music .... Noriko like?
   B: Classical music. She loves Yo-Yo Ma.
   A: Yeah, he's amazing. I like .... a lot.

Kings of Leon

PRONUNCIATION *Intonation in questions*

A ▶ Listen and practice. Yes/No questions usually have rising intonation. Wh-questions usually have falling intonation.

Do you like pop music?   What kind of music do you like?

B **PAIR WORK** Practice these questions.

Do you like TV?   What programs do you like?
Do you like video games?   What games do you like?
Do you play a musical instrument?   What instrument do you play?

6 SPEAKING *Entertainment survey*

A **GROUP WORK** Write five questions about entertainment and entertainers. Then ask and answer your questions in groups.

What kinds of . . . do you like?
   (music, TV programs, video games)
Do you like . . . ?
   (reggae, game shows, action movies)
Who's your favorite . . . ?
   (singer, actor, athlete)

B **GROUP WORK** Complete this information about your group. Ask any additional questions.

Our Group Favorites
What's your favorite kind of . . . ?
music ....
movie ....
TV program ....
What's your favorite . . . ?
song ....
movie ....
video game ....
Who's your favorite . . . ?
singer ....
actor ....
athlete ....

Utada Hikaru

reality show

Cristiano Ronaldo

3-D movie

C **CLASS ACTIVITY** Read your group's list to the class. Find out the class favorites.

7 LISTENING *Who's my date?*

A ▶ Listen to four people on a TV game show. Three men want to invite Linda on a date. What kinds of things do they like? Complete the chart.

	Music	Movies	TV programs
Bill	....	....	....
John	....	....	....
Tony	....	....	....
Linda	....	....	....

B **CLASS ACTIVITY** Who do you think is the best date for Linda? Why?

8 CONVERSATION *An invitation*

A ▶ Listen and practice.

Dave: I have tickets to the soccer match on Friday night. Would you like to go?

Susan: Thanks. I'd love to. What time does it start?

Dave: At 8:00.

Susan: That sounds great. So, do you want to have dinner at 6:00?

Dave: Uh, I'd like to, but I have to work late.

Susan: Oh, that's OK. Let's just meet at the stadium before the match, around 7:30.

Dave: OK. Why don't we meet at the gate?

Susan: That sounds fine. See you there.

B ▶ Listen to Dave and Susan at the soccer match. Which team does each person like?

9 GRAMMAR FOCUS

Would; verb + to + verb ▶

		Contraction
Would you **like to go** out on Friday?	**Would** you **like to go** to a soccer match?	**I'd** = I would
Yes, I **would**.	**I'd like to**, but I **have to work** late.	
Yes, I'**d love to**. Thanks.	**I'd like to**, but I **need to save** money.	
	I'd like to, but I **want to visit** my parents.	

A Respond to three invitations. Then write three invitations for the given responses.

1. A: I have tickets to the baseball game on Saturday. Would you like to go?
   B: ....

2. A: Would you like to come over for dinner tomorrow night?
   B: ....

3. A: Would you like to go to a pop concert with me this weekend?
   B: ....

4. A: ....
   ....
   B: Yes, I'd love to. Thank you!

5. A: ....
   ....
   B: Well, I'd like to, but I have to study.

6. A: ....
   ....
   B: Yes, I would. They're my favorite band.

B **PAIR WORK** Ask and answer the questions in part A. Give your own responses.

C **PAIR WORK** Think of three things you would like to do. Then invite a partner to do them with you. Your partner responds and asks follow-up questions like these:

When is it?   What time does it start?   When does it end?   Where is it?

10 WRITING A text message

A What does this text message say?

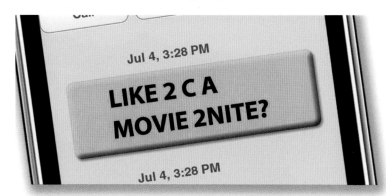

text message abbreviations			
M	= am	L8	= late
U	= you	W8	= wait
R	= are	GR8	= great
C	= see	THX	= thanks
4	= for	LUV	= love
2	= to	NITE	= night

B **GROUP WORK** Write a text message to each person in your group. Then exchange messages. Write a response to each message.

11 INTERCHANGE 4 Are you free this weekend?

Make weekend plans with your classmates. Go to Interchange 4 on page 118.

12 READING

Fergie of the Black Eyed Peas

Scan the article and look at the pictures. In what year did each event take place?

She has many hit singles and several Grammy awards with her band the Black Eyed Peas. She has fans all over the world. She's a singer, a rapper, a songwriter, a fashion designer, and an actress. Her name is Stacy Ann Ferguson, but her fans call her Fergie.

Here are some highlights of Fergie's life and career.

- ▶ **1975** Fergie is born on March 27 in California.
- ▶ **1984** Fergie starts acting, doing the voice of Sally in the *Peanuts* cartoons. She also stars in the popular TV show *Kids Incorporated,* with actress Jennifer Love Hewitt.
- ▶ **1991** Fergie forms the all-female band Wild Orchid.
- ▶ **2003** Fergie records a song with the band Black Eyed Peas. The band likes her, and she records five more songs on the album.
- ▶ **2004** Fergie joins the Black Eyed Peas.
- ▶ **2005** Fergie and the Black Eyed Peas win their first Grammy award for "Let's Get It Started."
- ▶ **2006** Fergie makes a solo album and has six big hits. "Big Girls Don't Cry" is her first worldwide number one single.
- ▶ **2008** Fergie records "That Ain't Cool" with Japanese R&B singer Kumi Koda. She becomes famous in Japan.
- ▶ **2009** Fergie acts and sings in the movie *Nine*.
- ▶ **2010** Fergie and the Black Eyed Peas perform five songs at the 2010 World Cup celebration concert in South Africa.

Fergie says she's the "luckiest girl in the world." Why? Her song "Glamorous" says it all: "All the fans, I'd like to thank. Thank you really though, 'cause I remember yesterday when I dreamed about the days when I'd rock on MTV...."

▲ performing at the World Cup

▲ on the TV show *Kids Incorporated*

▲ on stage with the Black Eyed Peas

A Read the article. Then number these sentences from 1 (first event) to 8 (last event).

.... a. She sings at the World Cup concert.
.... b. She is born in California.
.... c. She acts and sings in a movie.
.... d. Her band wins its first Grammy.
.... e. She forms her first band.
.... f. She is on TV with Jennifer Love Hewitt.
.... g. She becomes very popular in Japan.
.... h. She has her first worldwide number one song.

B **PAIR WORK** Who is your favorite musician? What do you know about his or her life?

Units 3–4 Progress check

SELF-ASSESSMENT

How well can you do these things? Check (✔) the boxes.

I can	Very well	OK	A little
Give and understand information about prices (Ex. 1)	☐	☐	☐
Say what I like and dislike (Ex. 1, 2, 3)	☐	☐	☐
Explain what I like or dislike about something (Ex. 2)	☐	☐	☐
Describe and compare objects and possessions (Ex. 2)	☐	☐	☐
Make and respond to invitations (Ex. 4)	☐	☐	☐

1 LISTENING *Weekend sale*

A ▶ Listen to a commercial for Dave's Discount Store. Circle the correct prices.

DAVE'S DISCOUNT STORE

leather pants
$19
$90

wool pants
$15
$50

silk shirt
$14
$40

cotton shirt
$18
$80

laptop computer
$1,015
$1,050

desktop computer
$813
$830

B **PAIR WORK** What do you think of the items in part A? Give your own opinions.

2 ROLE PLAY *Shopping trip*

Student A: Choose things from Exercise 1 for your family. Ask for Student B's opinion.

Student B: Help Student A choose presents for his or her family.

> A: I want to buy a computer for my parents. Which one do you like better?
> B: Well, I like the laptop better. It's nicer, and . . .

Change roles and try the role play again.

SURVEY *Likes and dislikes*

A Write answers to these questions.

	Me	My classmate
When do you usually watch TV?	....	....
What kinds of TV programs do you like?	....	....
Do you like game shows?	....	....
Do you listen to the radio?	....	....
Who is your favorite singer?	....	....
What do you think of heavy metal?	....	....
What is your favorite movie?	....	....
Do you like musicals?	....	....
What kinds of movies do you dislike?	....	....

B **CLASS ACTIVITY** Find someone who has the same answers. Go around the class. Write a classmate's name only once!

4 **SPEAKING** *What an excuse!*

A Make up three invitations to interesting activities. Write them on cards.

> *I want to see the frog races tomorrow. They're at the park at 2:00. Would you like to go?*

B Write three response cards. One is an acceptance card, and two are refusals. Think of silly or unusual excuses.

That sounds great! What time do you want to meet?	*I'd like to, but I have to wash my cat tomorrow.*	*I'd love to, but I want to take my bird to a singing contest.*

C **GROUP WORK** Shuffle the invitation cards together and the response cards together. Take three cards from each pile. Then invite people to do the things on your invitation cards. Use the response cards to accept or refuse.

WHAT'S NEXT?

Look at your Self-assessment again. Do you need to review anything?

5 I come from a big family.

1 WORD POWER Family

A Look at Sam's family tree. How are these people related to him? Add the words to the family tree.

cousin
daughter
father
grandmother
niece
sister-in-law
uncle
wife

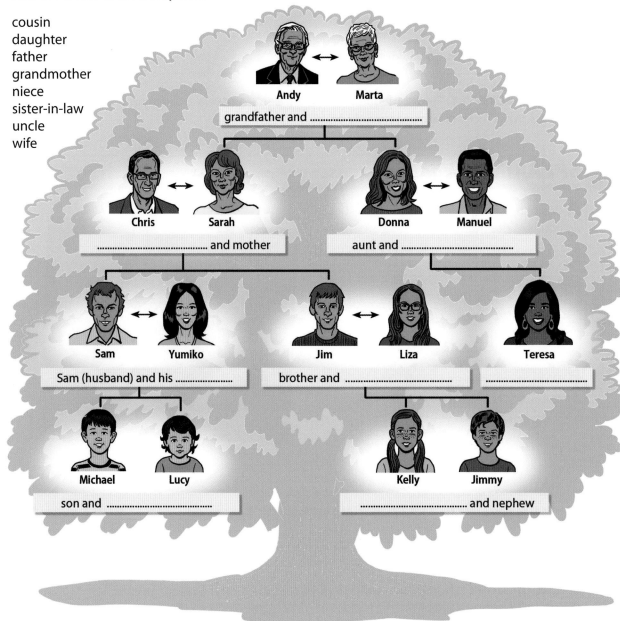

Andy ↔ Marta
grandfather and ....

Chris ↔ Sarah
.... and mother

Donna ↔ Manuel
aunt and ....

Sam ↔ Yumiko
Sam (husband) and his ....

Jim ↔ Liza
brother and ....

Teresa
....

Michael   Lucy
son and ....

Kelly   Jimmy
.... and nephew

B Draw your family tree (or a friend's family tree). Then take turns talking about your families. Ask follow-up questions to get more information.

A: There are five people in my family. I have two brothers and a sister.
B: How old is your sister?

2 LISTENING *How are they related?*

▶ Listen to four conversations about famous people. How is the second person related to the first person?

1.

Chris
Martin

Gwyneth
Paltrow

....

2.

Francis
Ford
Coppola

Nicholas
Cage

....

3.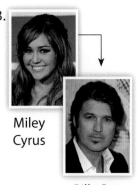

Miley
Cyrus

Billy Ray
Cyrus

....

4.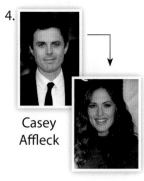

Casey
Affleck

Jennifer
Garner

....

3 CONVERSATION *Asking about families*

A ▶ Listen and practice.

Rita: Tell me about your brother and sister, Sue.
Sue: Well, my sister works for the government.
Rita: Oh, what does she do?
Sue: I'm not sure. She's working on a very secret project right now.
Rita: Wow! And what about your brother?
Sue: He's a wildlife photographer.
Rita: What an interesting family! Can I meet them?
Sue: Sure, but not now. My sister's away. She's not working in the United States this month.
Rita: And your brother?
Sue: He's traveling in the Amazon.

B ▶ Listen to the rest of the conversation. Where do Rita's parents live? What do they do?

4 PRONUNCIATION *Intonation in statements*

A ▶ Listen and practice. Notice that statements usually have falling intonation.

He's traveling in the Amazon.   She's working on a very secret project.

B PAIR WORK Practice the conversation in Exercise 3 again. Pay attention to the intonation in the statements.

I come from a big family. ▪ **31**

Present continuous ▶

Are you **living** at home now?	Yes, I **am**.	No, I**'m not**.
Is your sister **working** for the government?	Yes, she **is**.	No, she**'s not**./No, she **isn't**.
Are Ed and Jill **taking** classes this year?	Yes, they **are**.	No, they**'re not**./No, they **aren't**.

Where **are** you **working** now? — I**'m not working**. I need a job.
What **is** your brother **doing**? — He**'s traveling** in the Amazon.
What **are** your friends **doing** these days? — They**'re studying** for their exams.

A Complete these phone conversations using the present continuous.

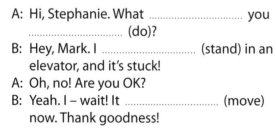

A: Hi, Stephanie. What .... you .... (do)?
B: Hey, Mark. I .... (stand) in an elevator, and it's stuck!
A: Oh, no! Are you OK?
B: Yeah. I – wait! It .... (move) now. Thank goodness!

A: Marci, how .... you and Justin .... (enjoy) your shopping trip?
B: We .... (have) a lot of fun.
A: .... your brother .... (spend) a lot of money?
B: No, Mom. He .... (buy) only one or two things. That's all!

B PAIR WORK Practice the phone conversations with a partner.

6 *DISCUSSION* *Is anyone...?*

GROUP WORK Ask your classmates about people in their families. What are they doing? Ask follow-up questions to get more information.

A: Is anyone in your family traveling right now?
B: Yes, my dad is. He's in South Korea.
C: What's he doing there?

topics to ask about	
traveling	going to high school or college
living abroad	moving to a new home
taking a class	studying a foreign language

7 **INTERCHANGE 5** *Family facts*

Find out about your classmates' families. Go to Interchange 5 on page 119.

8 **SNAPSHOT**

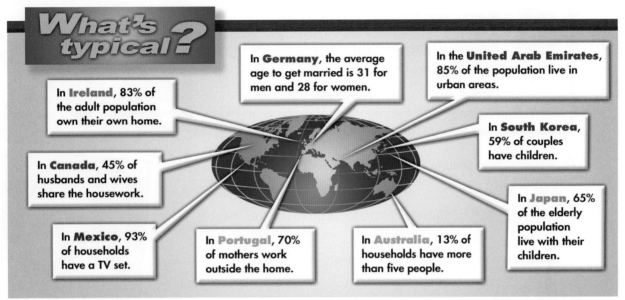

What's typical?

In **Germany**, the average age to get married is 31 for men and 28 for women.

In the **United Arab Emirates**, 85% of the population live in urban areas.

In **Ireland**, 83% of the adult population own their own home.

In **South Korea**, 59% of couples have children.

In **Canada**, 45% of husbands and wives share the housework.

In **Japan**, 65% of the elderly population live with their children.

In **Mexico**, 93% of households have a TV set.

In **Portugal**, 70% of mothers work outside the home.

In **Australia**, 13% of households have more than five people.

Source: nationmaster.com

Which facts surprise you? Why?
Which facts seem like positive things? Which seem negative?
How do you think your country compares?

9 **CONVERSATION** *Is that typical?*

A ▶ Listen and practice.

Marcos: How many brothers and sisters do you have, Mei-li?
Mei-li: Actually, I'm an only child.
Marcos: Really?
Mei-li: Yeah, a lot of families in China have only one child these days.
Marcos: I didn't know that.
Mei-li: What about you, Marcos?
Marcos: I come from a big family. I have three brothers and two sisters.
Mei-li: Wow! Is that typical in Peru?
Marcos: I'm not sure. Many families are smaller these days. But big families are great because you get a lot of birthday presents!

B ▶ Listen to the rest of the conversation. What does Mei-li like about being an only child?

10 GRAMMAR FOCUS

Quantifiers ▶

100%	**All**	
	Nearly all	families have only one child.
	Most	
	Many	
	A lot of	families are smaller these days.
	Some	
	Not many	couples have more than one child.
	Few	
0%	**No one**	gets married before the age of 18.

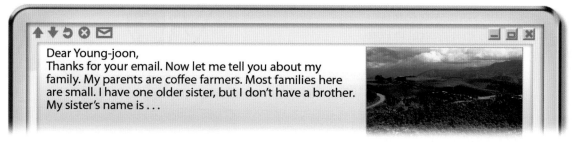

A Rewrite these sentences using quantifiers. Then compare with a partner.

1. In the U.S., 75% of high school students go to college.

   ....

2. Seven percent of the people in Brazil are age 65 or older.

   ....

3. In India, 0% of the people vote before the age of 18.

   ....

4. Forty percent of the people in Sweden live alone.

   ....

5. In Singapore, 23% of the people speak English at home.

   ....

B **PAIR WORK** Rewrite the sentences in part A so that they are true about your country.

> In . . . , many high school students go to college.

11 WRITING An email about your family

A Write an email to your e-pal about your family.

Dear Young-joon,
Thanks for your email. Now let me tell you about my family. My parents are coffee farmers. Most families here are small. I have one older sister, but I don't have a brother. My sister's name is . . .

B **GROUP WORK** Take turns reading your emails. Ask questions to get more information.

Stay-at-Home Dads

Read the title of the article. Then check (✓) the question you think the interviews will answer. ■ Why do men decide to stay at home with their children? ■ What happens when both parents work?

Families in the U.S. are changing. One important change is that many fathers are staying home with their children. They take care of the kids, and their wives go to work. *Modern Family* magazine asked three stay-at-home dads the question "What's it like being a stay-at-home dad?"

William Chan

I'm having a great time! When the kids are in school, I do housework. Our youngest child goes to school part-time. When I pick her up, I love the one-on-one time with her. Then, when my two sons get home from school, we all play together. Why do I stay home? Well, I wasn't happy at my job. It was pretty stressful, in fact.

Daniel Evans

It's a challenge. We have two young children. They don't go to school yet. I never have time for myself! That's not easy. But my kids are growing up so fast. I really want to spend time with them when they're young. Also, my wife loves her job. I think most stay-at-home dads say the same thing: It's hard, but it's worth it.

Roberto Garcia

In my neighborhood, there aren't many dads in the park with their kids on weekdays. Nearly all of the parents are moms. I had a stressful job before and didn't have a lot of free time. I hated it. We have a daughter, and now I'm spending more time with her. I love that. I'm enjoying my freedom from work, but I'm also working very hard!

A Read the interviews. Check (✓) the correct names.

Who . . . ?	William	Daniel	Roberto
1. has more than two children	☐	☐	☐
2. has an only child	☐	☐	☐
3. had a stressful career	☐	☐	☐
4. thinks it's hard to stay at home	☐	☐	☐
5. has a wife with a great job	☐	☐	☐

B PAIR WORK What do the dads like about staying at home? What challenges are they having? What are some other reasons dads stay at home?

6 How often do you exercise?

1 SNAPSHOT

The Top Five Sports and Fitness Activities in the United States

Sports	Fitness Activities
☐ basketball	☐ walking
☐ baseball	☐ weight training
☐ soccer	☐ treadmill
☐ football	☐ stretching
☐ softball	☐ jogging

Source: SGMA International, *Sports Participation in America*

Do people in your country enjoy any of these sports or activities?
Check (✓) the sports or fitness activities you enjoy.
Make a list of other sports or activities you do. Then compare with the class.

2 WORD POWER *Sports and exercise*

A Which of these activities are popular with the following age groups?
Check (✓) the activities. Then compare with a partner.

	Children	Teens	Young adults	Middle-aged people	Older people
aerobics	☐	☐	☐	☐	☐
bicycling	☐	☐	☐	☐	☐
bowling	☐	☐	☐	☐	☐
golf	☐	☐	☐	☐	☐
karate	☐	☐	☐	☐	☐
swimming	☐	☐	☐	☐	☐
tennis	☐	☐	☐	☐	☐
volleyball	☐	☐	☐	☐	☐
yoga	☐	☐	☐	☐	☐

B **PAIR WORK** Which activities in part A are used with *do, go,* or *play*?

do aerobics	*go bicycling*	*play golf*

3 CONVERSATION *I hardly ever exercise.*

A ▶ Listen and practice.

Marie: You're really fit, Paul. Do you exercise a lot?
 Paul: Well, I almost always get up early, and
        I lift weights for an hour.
Marie: Seriously?
 Paul: Sure. And then I often go swimming.
Marie: Wow! How often do you exercise like that?
 Paul: About five times a week. What about you?
Marie: Oh, I hardly ever exercise. I usually just
        watch TV in my free time. I guess I'm a
        real couch potato!

B ▶ Listen to the rest of the conversation.
What else does Paul do in his free time?

4 GRAMMAR FOCUS

Adverbs of frequency ▶

How often do you exercise?	Do you **ever** watch TV in the evening?		
I lift weights **every day**.	Yes, I **often** watch TV after dinner.	100%	**always**
I go jogging **once a week**.	I **sometimes** watch TV before bed.		**almost always**
I play soccer **twice a month**.	**Sometimes** I watch TV before bed.*		**usually**
I swim about **three times a year**.	I **hardly ever** watch TV.		**often**
I don't exercise very **often/much**.	No, I **never** watch TV.		**sometimes**
Usually I exercise before work.*			**hardly ever**
			almost never
	*Usually and *sometimes* can begin a sentence.	0%	**never**

A Put the adverbs in the correct place. Then practice with a partner.

1. A: Do you play sports? (ever)
   B: Sure. I play soccer. (twice a week)

2. A: What do you do on Saturday mornings? (usually)
   B: Nothing much. I sleep until noon. (almost always)

3. A: Do you do aerobics at the gym? (often)
   B: No, I do aerobics. (hardly ever)

4. A: Do you exercise on Sundays? (always)
   B: No, I exercise on Sundays. (never)

5. A: What do you do after class? (usually)
   B: I go out with my classmates. (about three
      times a week)

B **PAIR WORK** Take turns asking the questions in
part A. Give your own information when answering.

How often do you exercise? ▪ **37**

5 PRONUNCIATION Intonation with direct address

A Listen and practice. Notice these statements with direct address. There is usually falling intonation and a pause before the name.

You're really fit, Paul.   You look tired, Marie.   I feel great, Dr. Lee.

B **PAIR WORK** Write four statements using direct address. Then practice them.

6 SPEAKING Fitness poll

A **GROUP WORK** Take a poll in your group. One person takes notes. Take turns asking each person these questions.

1. Do you have a regular fitness program? How often do you exercise?

2. Do you ever go to a gym? How often do you go? What do you do there?

3. Do you play any sports? Which ones? How often do you play them?

4. Do you ever take long walks? How often? Where do you go?

5. What else do you do to keep fit?

B **GROUP WORK** Study the results of the poll. Who in your group has a good fitness program?

7 LISTENING In the evening

A Listen to three people discuss what they like to do in the evening. Complete the chart.

	Activity	How often?
Justin	....	....
Carrie	....	....
Marcos	....	....

B Listen again. Who is most similar to you – Justin, Carrie, or Marcos?

8 DISCUSSION *Sports and athletes*

GROUP WORK Take turns asking and answering these questions.

Who's your favorite male athlete? Why?
Who's your favorite female athlete? Why?
Who are three famous athletes in your country?
What's your favorite sports team? Why?
Do you ever watch sports on TV? Which ones?
Do you ever watch sports live? Which ones?
What are two sports you don't like?
What sport or activity do you want to try?

9 WRITING *About favorite activities*

A Write about your favorite activities. Include one activity that is false.

> I love to exercise! I usually work out every day. I get up early in the morning and go jogging for about 30 minutes. Then I often go to the gym and do yoga. Sometimes I play tennis in the afternoon. I play . . .

B **GROUP WORK** Take turns reading your descriptions. Can you guess the false information?

"You don't play tennis in the afternoon. Right?"

10 CONVERSATION *I'm a real fitness freak.*

A Listen and practice.

Ruth: You're in great shape, Keith.
Keith: Thanks. I guess I'm a real fitness freak.
Ruth: How often do you work out?
Keith: Well, I do aerobics twice a week. And I play tennis every week.
Ruth: Tennis? That sounds like a lot of fun.
Keith: Oh, do you want to play sometime?
Ruth: Uh, . . . how well do you play?
Keith: Pretty well, I guess.
Ruth: Well, all right. But I'm not very good.
Keith: No problem. I'll give you a few tips.

B Listen to Keith and Ruth after their tennis match. Who's the winner?

11 GRAMMAR FOCUS

 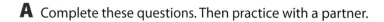
How often do you work out?
    Every day.
    Twice a week.
    Not very often.

How long do you spend at the gym?
    Thirty minutes a day.
    Two hours a week.
    About an hour on weekends.

How well do you play tennis?
    Pretty well.
    About average.
    Not very well.

How good are you at sports?
    Pretty good.
    OK.
    Not so good.

A Complete these questions. Then practice with a partner.

1. A: .... at volleyball?
   B: I guess I'm pretty good. I often play on weekends.

2. A: .... spend online?
   B: About an hour after dinner. I like to chat with my friends.

3. A: .... play chess?
   B: Once or twice a month. It's a good way to relax.

4. A: .... swim?
   B: Not very well. I need to take swimming lessons.

B GROUP WORK Take turns asking the questions in part A.
Give your own information when answering.

12 LISTENING *I'm terrible at sports.*

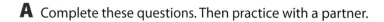 Listen to Dan, Jean, Sally, and Phil discuss sports and exercise.
Who is a couch potato? a fitness freak? a sports nut? a gym rat?

a couch potato	a fitness freak	a sports nut	a gym rat
1.	2.	3.	4. ....

13 INTERCHANGE 6 *Do you dance?*

Find out what your classmates can do. Go to Interchange 6 on page 120.

Health and Fitness Quiz

How healthy and fit do you think you are? Skim the questions below.
Then guess your health and fitness score from 0 (very unhealthy) to 50 (very healthy).

☺🍴 Your Food and Nutrition

1. How many meals do you eat each day? — **Points**
- Four or five small meals — 5
- Three meals — 3
- One or two big meals — 0

2. How often do you eat at regular times during the day?
- Almost always — 5
- Usually — 3
- Hardly ever — 0

3. How many servings of fruits or vegetables do you eat each day?
- Five or more — 5
- One to four — 3
- None — 0

4. How much junk food do you eat?
- Very little — 5
- About average — 3
- A lot — 0

5. Do you take vitamins?
- Yes, every day — 5
- Sometimes — 3
- No — 0

🚴 Your Fitness

6. How often do you exercise or play a sport? — **Points**
- Three or more days a week — 5
- One or two days a week — 3
- Never — 0

7. Which best describes your exercise program? — **Points**
- Both weight training and aerobic exercise — 5
- Either weight training or aerobic exercise — 3
- None — 0

8. How important is your fitness program to you?
- Very important — 5
- Fairly important — 3
- Not very important — 0

♡ Your Health

9. How often do you get a physical exam? — **Points**
- Once a year — 5
- Every two or three years — 3
- Rarely — 0

10. How often do you sleep well?
- Always — 5
- Usually or sometimes — 3
- Hardly ever or never — 0

Rate yourself

TOTAL POINTS
- **42 to 50:** Excellent job! Keep up the good work!
- **28 to 41:** Good! Your health and fitness are above average.
- **15 to 27:** Your health and fitness are a little below average.
- **14 or below:** You can improve your health and fitness.

A Take the quiz and add up your score. Is your score similar to your original guess? Do you agree with your quiz score? Why or why not?

B GROUP WORK Compare your scores. Who is the healthiest and fittest? What can you do to improve your health and fitness?

Units 5–6 Progress check

SELF-ASSESSMENT

How well can you do these things? Check (✓) the boxes.

I can	Very well	OK	A little
Ask about and describe present activities (Ex. 1, 2, 3)	☐	☐	☐
Describe family life (Ex. 3)	☐	☐	☐
Ask for and give personal information (Ex. 3)	☐	☐	☐
Give information about quantities (Ex. 3)	☐	☐	☐
Ask and answer questions about free time (Ex. 4)	☐	☐	☐
Ask and answer questions about routines and abilities (Ex. 4)	☐	☐	☐

1 LISTENING *What are they doing?*

A ⊙ Listen to people do different things. What are they doing? Complete the chart.

B **PAIR WORK** Compare your answers.

A: In number one, someone is watching TV.
B: I don't think so. I think someone is . . .

What are they doing?
1. ....
2. ....
3. ....
4. ....

2 GAME *Memory test*

GROUP WORK Choose a person in the room, but don't say who! Other students ask yes/no questions to guess the person.

A: I'm thinking of someone in the classroom.
B: Is it a woman?
A: Yes, it is.
C: Is she sitting in the front of the room?
A: No, she isn't.
D: Is she sitting in the back?
A: Yes, she is.
E: Is she wearing jeans?
A: No, she isn't.
B: Is it . . . ?

The student with the correct guess has the next turn.

SURVEY *Family life*

A **GROUP WORK** Add two more yes/no questions about family life to the chart. Then ask and answer the questions in groups. Write down the number of "yes" and "no" answers. (Remember to include yourself.)

	Number of "yes" answers	Number of "no" answers
1. Are you living with your family?	....	....
2. Do your parents both work?	....	....
3. Do you eat dinner with your family?	....	....
4. Are you working these days?	....	....
5. Are you married?	....	....
6. Do you have any children?	....	....
7.	....	....
8.	....	....

B **GROUP WORK** Write up the results of the survey. Then tell the class.

> 1. In our group, most people are living with their family.
> 2. Few of our parents both work.

4 **DISCUSSION** *Routines and abilities*

GROUP WORK Choose three questions. Then ask your questions in groups. When someone answers "yes," think of other questions to ask.

Do you ever . . . ?
- sing karaoke
- listen to English songs
- chat online
- do weight training
- play golf
- play video games
- cook for friends
- go swimming
- watch old movies

A: **Do you ever** sing karaoke?
B: Yes, I often do.
C: **What** song do you like to sing?
B: "I Love Rock 'n' Roll."
A: **When** do you sing karaoke?
B: In the evenings.
C: **How often** do you go?
B: Every weekend!
D: **How well** do you sing?
B: Not very well. But I have a lot of fun!

Yeaaaaaaaaaaaah!

WHAT'S NEXT?

Look at your Self-assessment again. Do you need to review anything?

7 We had a great time!

1 SNAPSHOT

The Top Eight Leisure-Time Activities in the United States

☐ read   ☐ watch TV   ☐ spend time with family   ☐ play sports

☐ go to the gym   ☐ use the computer   ☐ go fishing   ☐ go to the movies

Source: The Harris Poll

Check (✓) the activities you do in your free time.
List three other activities you do in your free time.
What are your favorite leisure-time activities?

2 CONVERSATION *Did you do anything special?*

A ▶ Listen and practice.

Rick: So, what did you do last weekend, Meg?
Meg: Oh, I had a great time. I went to a karaoke bar and sang with some friends on Saturday.
Rick: How fun! Did you go to Lucky's?
Meg: No, we didn't. We went to that new place downtown. How about you? Did you go anywhere?
Rick: No, I didn't go anywhere all weekend. I just stayed home and studied for today's Spanish test.
Meg: Our test is today? I forgot about that!
Rick: Don't worry. You always get an A.

B ▶ Listen to the rest of the conversation. What does Meg do on Sunday afternoons?

GRAMMAR FOCUS

Simple past ⊙

Did you **work** on Saturday?
    Yes, I **did**. I **worked** all day.
    No, I **didn't**. I **didn't work** at all.

Did you **go** anywhere last weekend?
    Yes, I **did**. I **went** to the movies.
    No, I **didn't**. I **didn't go** anywhere.

What **did** Rick **do** on Saturday?
He **stayed** home and **studied** for a test.

How **did** Meg **spend** her weekend?
She **went** to a karaoke bar and **sang**
    with some friends.

A Complete these conversations. Then practice with a partner.

1. A: .... you .... (stay) home on Saturday?
    B: No, I .... (call) my friend. We .... (drive)
       to a café for lunch.
2. A: How .... you .... (spend) your last birthday?
    B: I .... (have) a party. Everyone .... (enjoy) it,
       but the neighbors .... (not, like) the noise.
3. A: What .... you .... (do) last night?
    B: I .... (see) a 3-D movie at the Cineplex.
       I .... (love) it!
4. A: .... you .... (do) anything special over the weekend?
    B: Yes, I .... I .... (go) shopping. Unfortunately,
       I .... (spend) all my money. Now I'm broke!
5. A: .... you .... (go) out on Friday night?
    B: No, I .... I .... (invite) friends over,
       and I .... (cook) dinner for them.

regular verbs	
work	→ worked
invite	→ invited
study	→ studied
stop	→ stopped

irregular verbs	
do	→ **did**
drive	→ **drove**
have	→ **had**
go	→ **went**
sing	→ **sang**
see	→ **saw**
spend	→ **spent**

B **PAIR WORK** Take turns asking the questions in part A.
Give your own information when answering.

A: Did you stay home on Saturday?
B: No, I didn't. I went out with some friends.

4 PRONUNCIATION *Reduction of* did you

A ⊙ Listen and practice. Notice how **did you** is reduced in the
following questions.

[dɪdʒə]
Did you have a good time?

[wədɪdʒə]
What did you do last night?

[haʊdɪdʒə]
How did you like the movie?

B **PAIR WORK** Practice the questions in Exercise 3, part A again.
Pay attention to the pronunciation of **did you**.

5 WORD POWER *Chores and activities*

A Find two other words or phrases from the list that usually
go with each verb.

| a lot of fun | dancing | a good time | shopping | a vacation |
| the bed | the dishes | the laundry | a trip | a video |

do	my homework	....	....
go	online	....	....
have	a party	....	....
make	a phone call	....	....
take	a day off	....	....

B Circle the things you did last weekend. Then compare with a partner.

A: I went shopping with my friends. We had a good time.
B: I didn't have a very good time. I did the laundry and . . .

6 DISCUSSION *Any questions?*

GROUP WORK Take turns. One student
makes a statement about the weekend.
Other students ask questions. Each
student answers at least three questions.

A: I went dancing on Saturday night.
B: **Where** did you go?
A: To the Rock-it Club.
C: **Who** did you go with?
A: I went with my friends.
D: **What time** did you go?
A: We went around 10:00.

7 LISTENING *What did you do last night?*

A   Listen to John and Laura
describe what they did last night.
Check (✓) the correct information
about each person.

B   Listen again. Who had a
good time? Who didn't have a
good time? Why or why not?

Who . . . ?	John	Laura
went to a party	☐	☐
had a good meal	☐	☐
watched a video	☐	☐
met an old friend	☐	☐
got home late	☐	☐

8 INTERCHANGE 7 *Thinking back*

Play a board game. Go to Interchange 7 on page 121.

9 CONVERSATION *How was your vacation?*

A ▶ Listen and practice.

Celia: Hi, Don. How was your vacation?
Don: It was excellent! I went to Hawaii with my cousin. We had a great time.
Celia: Lucky you. How long were you there?
Don: About a week.
Celia: Fantastic! Was the weather OK?
Don: Not really. It was cloudy a lot. But we went surfing every day. The waves were amazing.
Celia: So, what was the best thing about the trip?
Don: Well, something incredible happened. . . .

B ▶ Listen to the rest of the conversation. What happened?

10 GRAMMAR FOCUS

> ### Past of be ▶
>
> | | | |
> |---|---|---|
> | **Were** you in Hawaii? | Yes, I **was**. | **Contractions** |
> | **Was** the weather OK? | No, it **wasn't**. | was**n't** = was not |
> | **Were** you and your cousin on vacation? | Yes, we **were**. | were**n't** = were not |
> | **Were** your parents there? | No, they **weren't**. | |
> | How long **were** you away? | I **was** away for a week. | |
> | How **was** your vacation? | It **was** excellent! | |

Complete these conversations. Then practice with a partner.

1. A: .... you in Los Angeles last weekend?
   B: No, I .... I .... in San Francisco.
   A: How .... it?
   B: It .... great! But it .... foggy and cool as usual.

2. A: How long .... your parents in Europe?
   B: They .... there for two weeks.
   A: .... they in London the whole time?
   B: No, they .... They also went to Paris.

3. A: .... you away last week?
   B: Yes, I .... in Istanbul.
   A: Really? How long .... you there?
   B: For almost a week. I .... there on business.

Golden Gate Bridge

We had a great time! ▪ **47**

11 DISCUSSION On vacation

A **GROUP WORK** Ask your classmates about their last vacations.
Ask these questions or your own ideas.

Where did you spend your last vacation?   What did you do?
How long was your vacation?   How was the weather?
Who were you with?   What would you like to do on your next vacation?

B **CLASS ACTIVITY** Who had an interesting vacation? Tell the class who and why.

12 WRITING An online post

A Read this online post.

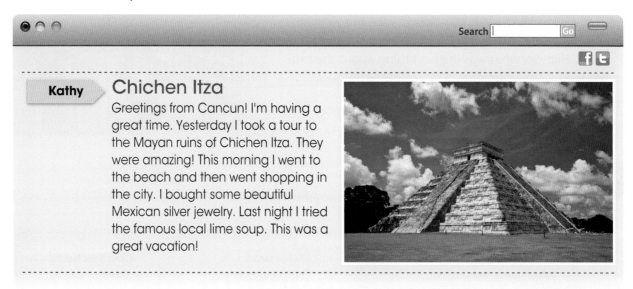

Search [   ] Go

Kathy ▷ Chichen Itza
Greetings from Cancun! I'm having a
great time. Yesterday I took a tour to
the Mayan ruins of Chichen Itza. They
were amazing! This morning I went to
the beach and then went shopping in
the city. I bought some beautiful
Mexican silver jewelry. Last night I tried
the famous local lime soup. This was a
great vacation!

B Write an online post to a partner about your last vacation. Then
exchange messages. Do you have any questions about the vacation?

13 LISTENING Welcome back.

A ▶ Listen to Jason and Barbara talk about their vacations.
Write where they went and what they did there.

	Where they went	What they did	Did they enjoy it?	
			Yes	**No**
Jason	....	....	☐	☐
Barbara	....	....	☐	☐

B ▶ Listen again. Did they enjoy their vacations? Check (✓) Yes or No.

Look at the pictures. What do you think each person did on his or her vacation?

Search [   ] Go

Rachel ▶ Terracotta Warriors

I arrived in China two weeks ago, but my trip is almost over! I'm with a group from the university. We stayed with families in Beijing for a week. We studied Mandarin every day, and I practiced a lot with my host family. Then my group took a trip to Xi'an. We saw the terracotta statues and learned about Chinese history. I'm tired, but I loved every minute of my trip.

Hee-jin ▶ Sanibel Island, Florida

I just spent a week at a yoga retreat in Florida. Every day, I did yoga, went for long walks on the beach, collected seashells, and ate great vegetarian food. I also learned how to play tennis. I feel fantastic! Now I'm going to visit friends in Miami for a few days. Click on my photo album to see more pictures!

Chris ▶ Greetings from Chile

Chile is amazing! I just returned from a trip to the Torres del Paine National Park. We took a plane to a boat to a bus to get to the park. I was with four other friends. We camped outside and hiked around the park for 10 days. I saw glaciers and lots of wildlife, including some pink flamingos. Now I'm back in Santiago for a week.

A Read the online posts. Then write the number of the post where each sentence could go.

.... It was a long trip, but I was so happy after we got there!
.... I really recommend this place – it's very relaxing.
.... I had a great trip, but now I need a vacation!

B **PAIR WORK** Answer these questions.

1. Which person had a fitness vacation?
2. Who learned a lot on vacation?
3. Who had a vacation that was full of adventure?
4. Which vacation sounds the most interesting to you? Why?

8 What's your neighborhood like?

1 WORD POWER Places

A Match the words and the definitions. Then ask and answer the questions with a partner.

What's a . . . ?	*It's a place where you . . .*
1. barbershop	a. wash and dry clothes
2. grocery store	b. buy food
3. laundromat	c. buy cards and paper
4. library	d. get a haircut
5. stationery store	e. see a movie or play
6. theater	f. make reservations for a trip
7. travel agency	g. borrow books

B PAIR WORK Write definitions for these places.

clothing store   drugstore   Internet café   music store   post office

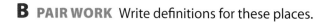

> It's a place where you find new fashions. (clothing store)

C GROUP WORK Read your definitions. Can others guess the places?

2 CONVERSATION I'm your new neighbor.

▶ Listen and practice.

Jack: Excuse me. I'm your new neighbor, Jack. I just moved in.

Mrs. Day: Oh. Yes?

Jack: I'm looking for a grocery store. Are there any around here?

Mrs. Day: Yes, there are some on Pine Street.

Jack: Oh, good. And is there a laundromat near here?

Mrs. Day: Well, I think there's one across from the shopping center.

Jack: Thank you.

Mrs. Day: By the way, there's a barbershop in the shopping center, too.

Jack: A barbershop?

3 GRAMMAR FOCUS

There is, there are; one, any, some ▶

Is there a laundromat near here?

    Yes, **there is**. There's **one** across from the shopping center.

    No, **there isn't**, but there's **one** next to the library.

Are there any grocery stores around here?

    Yes, **there are**. There are **some** nice stores on Pine Street.

    No, **there aren't**, but there are **some** on Third Avenue.

    No, **there aren't any** around here.

Prepositions

on
next to
near/close to
across from/opposite
in front of
in back of/behind
between
on the corner of

A Look at the map below. Write questions about these places.

a bank	an electronics store	grocery stores	hotels	a post office
a department store	gas stations	a gym	a pay phone	restaurants

> Is there a bank around here?
> Are there any gas stations on Main Street?

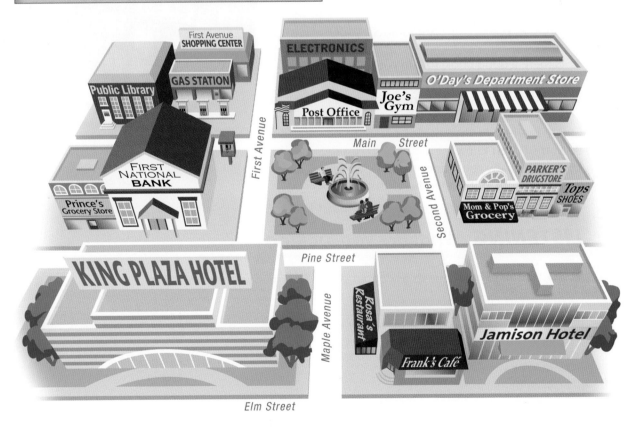

B **PAIR WORK** Ask and answer the questions you wrote in part A.

A: Is there a pay phone around here?
B: Yes, there is. There's one across from the gas station.

4 PRONUNCIATION *Reduction of there is/there are*

A Listen and practice. Notice how **there is** and **there are** are reduced in conversation, except for short answers.

Is there a laundromat near here?
  Yes, **there is. There's** one across from the shopping center.

Are there any grocery stores around here?
  Yes, **there are. There are** some on Pine Street.

B Practice the questions and answers in Exercise 3, part B again.

5 SPEAKING *My neighborhood*

GROUP WORK Take turns asking and answering questions about places like these in your neighborhood.

a bookstore   an Internet café
coffee shops   a karaoke bar
dance clubs   a library
drugstores   movie theaters
an electronics store a park
a gym   restaurants

A: Is there a good bookstore in your neighborhood?
B: Yes, there's an excellent one across from the park.
C: Are there any coffee shops?
B: Sorry, I don't know.
D: Are there any cool dance clubs?
B: I'm not sure, but I think there's one . . .

useful expressions
Sorry, I don't know.
I'm not sure, but I think . . .
Of course. There's one . . .

6 LISTENING *What are you looking for?*

A Listen to hotel guests ask about places to visit. Complete the chart.

Place	Location	Interesting?	
		Yes	No
Hard Rock Cafe	....	☐	☐
Science Museum	....	☐	☐
Aquarium	....	☐	☐

B **PAIR WORK** Which place sounds the most interesting to you? Why?

Common Complaints About Neighbors

Noise

☐ "My neighbor's dog barks all night."

☐ "My neighbor always listens to loud music."

Cleanliness

☐ "My neighbor puts his garbage in the hall."

☐ "There are always shoes outside my door."

Pets

☐ "My neighbor's cats go everywhere."

☐ "My neighbor has six dogs. It's like a zoo!"

Privacy

☐ "My neighbor's kids visit every day. It's too much!"

☐ "My neighbor always asks me for things."

Source: Based on information from njcooperator.com

Check (✔) the complaints you have about your neighbors.
What other complaints do you have about neighbors?
What do you do when you have complaints?

8 **CONVERSATION** *It's pretty safe.*

▶ Listen and practice.

Nick: How do you like your new apartment?

Pam: I love it. It's downtown, so it's very convenient.

Nick: Downtown? Is there much noise?

Pam: No, there isn't any. I live on the fifth floor.

Nick: How many restaurants are there near your place?

Pam: A lot. In fact, there's an excellent Korean place just around the corner.

Nick: What about parking?

Pam: Well, there aren't many parking garages. But I usually find a place on the street.

Nick: Is there much crime?

Pam: No, it's pretty safe. Hold on. That's my car alarm! I'll call you back later.

GRAMMAR FOCUS

Quantifiers; how many *and* how much ⏵

Count nouns	Noncount nouns
Are there **many restaurants**?	Is there **much crime**?
Yes, there are **a lot**.	Yes, there's **a lot**.
Yes, there are **a few**.	Yes, there's **a little**.
No, there are**n't many**.	No, there is**n't much**.
No, there are**n't any**.	No, there is**n't any**.
No, there are **none**.	No, there's **none**.
How many restaurants are there?	**How much** crime is there?
There are ten or twelve.	There's a lot of street crime.

A Write answers to these questions about your neighborhood. Then practice with a partner.

1. Is there much parking? ....
2. Are there many apartment buildings? ....
3. How much traffic is there? ....
4. How many dance clubs are there? ....
5. Is there much noise? ....
6. Are there many pay phones? ....
7. Is there much pollution? ....
8. How many swimming pools are there? ....

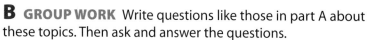

B **GROUP WORK** Write questions like those in part A about these topics. Then ask and answer the questions.

cafés   crime   parks   pollution   public transportation   schools   traffic lights

 INTERCHANGE 8 *Where am I?*

Play a guessing game. Go to Interchange 8 on page 122.

11 **WRITING** *A "roommate wanted" ad*

A Read these ads asking for roommates.

B Now write a "roommate wanted" ad. Use your real name at the end, but you can use a false phone number or email address.

C **CLASS ACTIVITY** Put your ads on the wall. Read the ads and choose one. Then find the person who wrote it. Ask questions to get more information.

Roommates 🏠 Wanted

Roommate needed to share large 3-bedroom apt. in nice neighborhood. Great park across the street. Only $440 a month! Parking available. Call Sheri or Jen at 352-555-8381.

Quiet student looking for roommate to share 2-bedroom house near university. Near public transportation. Pets OK. $550 a month plus utilities. Email Greg at g.adams@cup.com.

The World in One Neighborhood

Scan the article. Then check (✓) the countries that are not mentioned.
☐ Brazil ☐ China ☐ Greece ☐ India ☐ Spain ☐ Sudan ☐ Uruguay ☐ Vietnam

1 The sidewalks are crowded with people chatting in Cantonese. An Indian man sells spices from his corner shop. Brazilian music plays loudly from a café. Is it China? India? Brazil? No, it's Kensington Market, a neighborhood in Toronto, Canada. Kensington Market was once an Eastern European and Italian neighborhood, but the area changed along with its residents. First came the Portuguese, then East Asians, then people from Iran, Vietnam, Sudan, Brazil, the Caribbean, and the Middle East.

2 Today, the neighborhood is truly multicultural – you can hear more than 100 languages on its streets. New residents bring many new traditions. "What's really cool about Kensington is that as soon as you're in it, you feel as though you're not in Toronto anymore," says one resident. "I think what makes Kensington Market unique is that it's always changing," says another.

3 It isn't surprising that the area in and around Kensington Market is becoming a popular place to live. The rents are reasonable, the neighborhood is exciting, and it has good public transportation. There are apartments of every size and for every budget. It has inexpensive stores, fun cafés, fresh fruit and vegetable markets, and restaurants with almost every type of cuisine. As one resident says, "This place is the heart of Toronto."

A Read the article. Then write the number of each paragraph next to its main idea.

.... The residents and their traditions make Kensington Market a multicultural neighborhood.
.... People from all over the world live in Kensington Market.
.... The neighborhood has many good characteristics.

B Check (✓) the things you can find in Kensington Market.

☐ inexpensive stores   ☐ beautiful beaches   ☐ many different cultures
☐ big apartments   ☐ great markets   ☐ interesting old buildings
☐ good schools   ☐ good restaurants   ☐ good public transportation

C **PAIR WORK** Do you know of a neighborhood that is similar to Kensington Market? Describe it.

Units 7–8 Progress check

SELF-ASSESSMENT

How well can you do these things? Check (✓) the boxes.

I can	Very well	OK	A little
Understand descriptions of past events (Ex. 1)	☐	☐	☐
Describe events in the past (Ex. 1)	☐	☐	☐
Ask and answer questions about past activities (Ex. 2)	☐	☐	☐
Give and understand simple directions (Ex. 3)	☐	☐	☐
Talk about my neighborhood (Ex. 4)	☐	☐	☐

1 LISTENING *Frankie's weekend*

A ▶ A thief robbed a house on Saturday. A detective is questioning Frankie. The pictures show what Frankie really did on Saturday. Listen to their conversation. Are Frankie's answers true (**T**) or false (**F**)?

1:00 P.M.   T F   3:00 P.M.   T F   5:00 P.M.   T F   6:00 P.M.   T F   8:00 P.M.   T F   10:30 P.M.   T F

B **PAIR WORK** What did Frankie really do? Use the pictures to retell the story.

2 DISCUSSION *What do you remember?*

A Do you remember what you did yesterday? Check (✓) the things you did. Then add two other things you did.

☐ got up early   ☐ went shopping   ☐ did the dishes   ☐ went to bed late
☐ went to class   ☐ ate at a restaurant   ☐ watched TV   ☐ ....
☐ made phone calls   ☐ did the laundry   ☐ exercised   ☐ ....

B **GROUP WORK** Ask questions about each thing in part A.

A: Did you get up early yesterday?
B: No, I didn't. I got up at 10:00. I was very tired.

SPEAKING *The neighborhood*

A Create a neighborhood. Add five places to "My map."
Choose from this list.

a bank   cafés   a dance club   a drugstore   gas stations   a gym   a theater

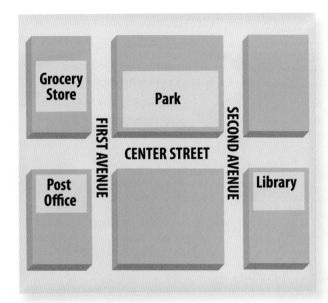

My map

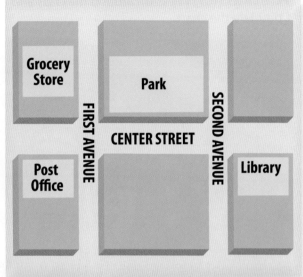

My partner's map

B **PAIR WORK** Ask questions about your partner's map. (But don't look!)
Draw the places on "My partner's map." Then compare your maps.

A: Are there any cafés in the neighborhood?
B: Yes, there's one on the corner of Center Street and First Avenue.

4 ROLE PLAY *What's it like?*

Student A: Imagine you are a visitor in Student B's neighborhood.
Ask questions about it.
Student B: Imagine a visitor wants to find out about your
neighborhood. Answer the visitor's questions.

A: How much crime is there?
B: There isn't much. It's a very safe neighborhood.
A: Is there much noise?
B: Well, yes, there's a lot. . . .

Change roles and try the role play again.

topics to ask about

crime
noise
parks
places to shop
pollution
public transportation
schools
traffic

WHAT'S NEXT?

Look at your Self-assessment again. Do you need to review anything?

Interchange activities

A **CLASS ACTIVITY** Go around the class and interview three classmates.
Complete the chart.

Excuse me, Lady Gaga.
Is Gaga your first name or
your last name?

	Classmate 1	Classmate 2	Classmate 3
What's your first name?			
What's your last name?			
What city are you from?			
When's your birthday?			
What's your favorite color?			
What are your hobbies?			

B **GROUP WORK** Compare your information. Then discuss these questions.

Who . . . ?

has an interesting first name   has the next birthday
has a common last name   likes black or white
is not from a big city   has an interesting hobby

interchange 2 *COMMON GROUND*

A CLASS ACTIVITY Answer these questions about yourself. Then interview two classmates. Write their names and the times they do each thing.

What time do you . . . ?	Me	Name	Name
get up during the week			
get up on weekends			
have breakfast			
leave for school or work			
get home during the week			
have dinner			
go to bed during the week			
go to bed on weekends			

B PAIR WORK Whose schedule is similar to yours? Tell your partner.

A: Keiko and I have similar schedules. We both get up at 6:00 and have breakfast at 7:00.
B: I leave for work at 7:30, but Jeff leaves for school at . . .

useful expressions

We both . . . at . . .
We . . . at different times.
My schedule is different from my two classmates' schedules.

Student A

A You want to sell these things. Write your "asking price" for each item.

TV
asking price: ....
sold for: ....

speakers
asking price: ....
sold for: ....

lamp
asking price: ....
sold for: ....

watch
asking price: ....
sold for: ....

Student B

A You want to sell these things. Write your "asking price" for each item.

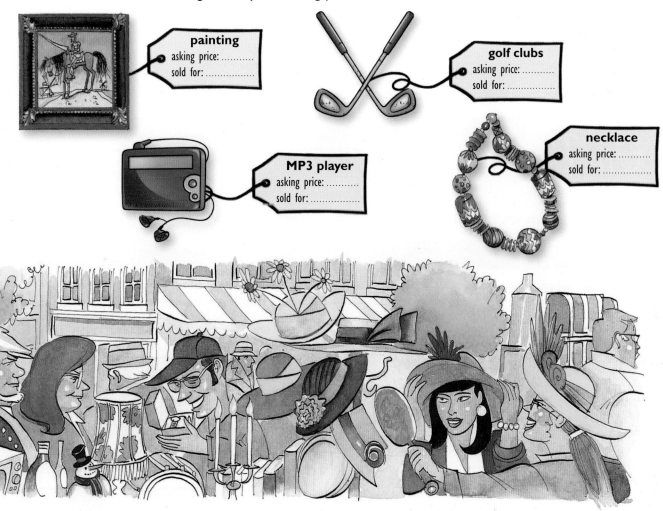

painting
asking price: ....
sold for: ....

golf clubs
asking price: ....
sold for: ....

MP3 player
asking price: ....
sold for: ....

necklace
asking price: ....
sold for: ....

Students A and B

B **PAIR WORK** Now choose three things you want to buy. Get the best price for each one. Then write what each item "sold for" on the price tag.

A: How much is the lamp?
B: It's only $30.
A: Wow! That's expensive!
B: Well, how about $25?
A: No. That's still too much. I'll give you $20 for it.
B: Sold! It's yours.

C **GROUP WORK** Compare your earnings in groups. Who made the most money at the flea market?

A Write two things you need to do this weekend. Include the times.

Saturday	Sunday
....	....
....	....

B Read the events page from your city's website. Choose three things you'd like to do.

On The Town

HOME
Log In
Register
Contact Us

Search the Calendar
What do you want to do?
GO

RESTAURANTS | LATE NIGHT | MUSIC | THEATER | MUSEUMS | OUTDOORS | KIDS | MOVIES | CALENDAR

TOP PICKS What's on this weekend

Saturday, May 21

Community Art Fair
See the work of local artists at the Community Art Fair! More than 200 artists, plus food, drinks, and music. Fun for the whole family!
11:00–5:00

Play Tennis!
Free tennis lessons for all ages. Central Park Tennis Courts. Bring a partner!
2:00–4:00

Bike Now's Ride Around the City
Once a year, this group organizes a bike ride around the city. Free food and drinks for cyclists from local restaurants.
Ride starts at 4:30.

Movies at Green Park
This Saturday's movie: *Avatar.* Bring your dinner, sit on the grass, and enjoy a movie under the stars.
Movie starts at 8:30. **MORE**

Sunday, May 22

Concerts on the River
Come hear your favorite music next to the White River. A different kind of music from a different country every week.
Concert starts at 1:00.

Chess in the Park
Bring a partner or find a partner at the city's biggest chess-a-thon. All levels and ages welcome. City Park, next to Park Café.
2:00–7:00

Free Tango Lessons
Learn to dance the tango! Live music and dancing. All levels. Beginners welcome. Center Street Activity Center.
5:30–7:00

City Baseball League
Green Park Team vs. the Lions. Come cheer for your favorite team! Come early to win prizes for the biggest fans!
Game at 7:30 **MORE**

C **GROUP WORK** Take turns inviting your classmates to the events. Say yes to one invitation and no to two invitations. Give a polite excuse.

A: Would you like to play tennis on Saturday? We can play from 2:00 to 4:00.
B: I'd like to, but I can't. I have to clean my room on Saturday afternoon.
A: Well, are you free in the morning?

A **CLASS ACTIVITY** Go around the class and find this information.
Write a classmate's name only once. Ask follow-up questions of your own.

Find someone	Name
1. who is an only child **"Do you have any brothers or sisters?"**	....
2. who has two brothers **"How many brothers do you have?"**	....
3. who has two sisters **"How many sisters do you have?"**	....
4. whose brother or sister is living abroad **"Are any of your brothers or sisters living abroad?"**	....
5. who lives with his or her grandparents **"Do you live with your grandparents?"**	....
6. who has a grandparent still working **"Is your grandmother or grandfather still working?"**	....
7. who has a family member with an unusual job **"Does anyone in your family have an unusual job?"**	....
8. whose mother or father is studying English **"Is either of your parents studying English?"**	....

B **GROUP WORK** Compare your information.

DO YOU DANCE?

A **CLASS ACTIVITY** Does anyone in your class do these things?
How often and how well? Go around the class and find one person
for each activity.

	Name	How often?	How well?
dance			
play an instrument			
sing			
act			
tell jokes			
do gymnastics			
do magic tricks			

A: Do you dance?
B: Yes, I do.
A: How often do you go dancing?
B: Every weekend.
A: Really? And how well do you dance?

B **GROUP WORK** Imagine there's a talent show this weekend.
Who do you want to enter? Choose three people from your class.
Explain your choices.

A: Let's enter Adam in the talent show.
B: Why Adam?
A: Because he dances very well.
C: Yes, he does. And Yvette is very good at playing the guitar.
    Let's enter her, too!

GROUP WORK Play the board game. Follow these instructions.

1. Use small pieces of paper with your initials on them as markers.
2. Take turns by tossing a coin: If the coin lands face up, move two spaces. If the coin lands face down, move one space.
3. When you land on a space, answer the question. Answer any follow-up questions.
4. If you land on "Free question," another player asks you any question.

A: I'll go first. Last night, I met my best friend.
B: Oh, yeah? Where did you go?
A: We went to the movies.

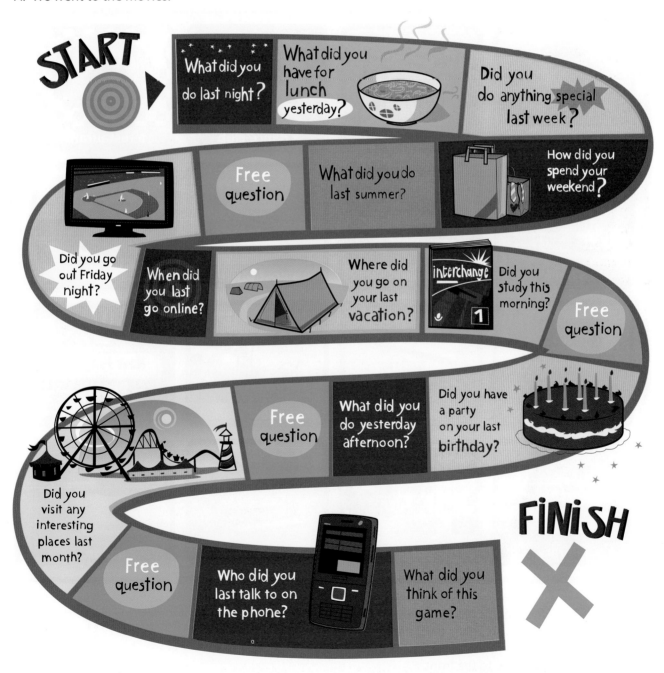

CLASS ACTIVITY Play a guessing game. Follow these instructions.

1. Get into two teams, A and B. One student from each team goes to the front of the class.
2. These two students choose a location and give four clues, using *There is/are* plus a quantifier.
3. The first student to guess the location correctly joins his or her teammate at the front.
4. The new student chooses a different location and gives clues. His or her team answers.
5. The first team with all of its members in the front wins.

A: There isn't any food in this place. There's a lot of coffee. There are a few computers. There are many emails. Where am I?
B: In an Internet café!
A: Correct! Now you come to the front.

Notes

Grammar plus

Unit 1

1 Statements with *be*; possessive adjectives (page 3)

▶ Don't confuse contractions of *be* with possessive adjectives: **You're** a student. **Your** class is English 1. (NOT: ~~You're class is English 1.~~) **He's** my classmate. **His** name is Roberto. (NOT: ~~He's name is Roberto.~~)

Circle the correct words.

1. This (is) / **are** Delia Rios. **She's / Her** a new student from Peru.
2. My name **am / is** Sergio. **I'm / He's** from Brazil.
3. My brother and I **is / are** students here. **Our / We're** names are Dave and Jeff.
4. **He's / His** Yoshi. **He's / His** 19 years old.
5. **They're / Their** in my English class. **It's / Its** a big class.

2 Wh-questions with *be* (page 4)

▶ Use *What* to ask about things: **What's** in your bag? Use *Where* to ask about places: **Where's** your friend from? Use *Who* to ask about people: **Who's** your teacher? Use *What . . . like?* to ask for a description: **What's** your friend **like**?

Match the questions with the answers.

1. Who's that? ....f....
2. Where's your teacher? ....
3. What are your friends like? ....
4. Where's she from? ....
5. Who are they? ....
6. What's his name? ....

a. They're really nice.
b. She's from Japan.
c. They're my brother and sister.
d. His name is Carlos.
e. He's in class.
f. That's our new classmate.

3 Yes/No questions and short answers with *be* (page 5)

▶ Use short answers to answer yes/no questions. Don't use contractions with short answers with *Yes*: **Are you** from Mexico? Yes, **I am**. (NOT: ~~Yes, I'm.~~)

Complete the conversations.

1. A: _Are they_ in your class?
   B: No, ... They're in English 2.
2. A: Hi! .... in this class?
   B: Yes, ... I'm a new student here.
3. A: .... from the United States?
   B: No, ... We're from Montreal, Canada.
4. A: Hi, Sonia. .... free?
   B: No, ... I'm on my way to class.
5. A: That's the new student. .... from Puerto Rico?
   B: No, ... He's from Costa Rica.
6. A: .... from Thailand?
   B: Yes, ... She's from Bangkok.

Unit 2

1 Simple present Wh-questions and statements (page 10)

Statements
▶ Verbs with he/she/it end in –s: He/She **walks** to school. BUT I/You/We/They **walk** to school.
▶ *Have, go,* and *do* are irregular with he/she/it: She **has** a class at 1:00. He **goes** to school at night. She **does** her homework before school.

Wh-questions
▶ Use *does* in questions with he/she/it and *do* with all the others: Where *does* he/she/it live? Where *do* I/you/we/they live?
▶ Don't add –s to the verb: Where does she **live**? (NOT: ~~Where does she lives?~~)

Complete the conversations with the correct form of the verbs in parentheses.

1. A: I ......*have*...... (have) good news! Dani .... (have) a new job.
   B: How .... she .... (like) it?
   A: She .... (love) it. The hours are great.
   B: What time .... she .... (start)?
   A: She .... (start) at nine and .... (finish) at five.
2. A: What .... you .... (do)?
   B: I'm a teacher.
   A: What .... you .... (teach)?
   B: I .... (teach) Spanish and English.
   A: Really? My sister .... (teach) English, too.

2 Time expressions (page 12)

▶ Use *in* with *the morning/afternoon/evening*. Us *at* with *night*: He goes to school **in** the afternoon and works **at** night. BUT: **on** *Friday night*.
▶ Use *at* with clock times: She gets up **at** 7:00.
▶ Use *on* with days: He gets up early **on** weekdays. She has class **on** Mondays.

Complete the conversation with time expressions from the box. You can use some words more than once.

at	early	in	on	until

A: How's your new job?
B: I love it, but the hours are difficult. I start work .... 7:30 A.M., and I work .... 3:30.
A: That's interesting! I work the same hours, but I work .... night. I start .... 7:30 .... the evening and finish .... 3:30 .... the morning.
B: Wow! What time do you get up?
A: Well, I get home .... 4:30 and go to bed .... 5:30. And I sleep .... 2:00. But I only work .... weekends, so it's OK. What about you?
B: Oh, I work .... Monday, Wednesday, and Friday. And I get up .... – around 6:00 A.M.

Unit 3

1 Demonstratives; *one, ones* (page 17)

> ▶ With singular nouns, use *this* for a thing that is nearby and *that* for a thing that is not nearby: How much is **this** cap here? How much is **that** cap over there?
>
> ▶ With plural nouns, use *these* for things that are nearby and *those* for things that are not nearby: How much are **these** earrings here? How much are **those** earrings over there?
>
> ▶ Use *one* to replace a singular noun: I like the red <u>hat</u>. → I like the red **one**. Use *ones* to replace plural nouns: I like the green <u>bags</u>. → I like the green **ones**.

Circle the correct words.

1. A: Excuse me. How much are **this / these** shoes?
   B: **It's / They're** $279.
   A: And how much is **this / that** bag over there?
   B: **It's / They're** only $129.
   A: And are the two gray **one / ones** $129, too?
   B: No. **That / Those** are only $119.
   A: Oh! **This / That** store is really expensive.

2. A: Can I help you?
   B: Yes, please. I really like **these / those** jeans over there. How much **is it / are they**?
   A: Which **one / ones**? Do you mean **this / these**?
   B: No, the black **one / ones**.
   A: Let me look. Oh, **it's / they're** $35.99.
   B: That's not bad. And how much is **this / that** sweater here?
   A: **It's / They're** only $9.99.

2 Preferences; comparisons with adjectives (page 20)

> ▶ With adjectives of one or two syllables, add *–er* to form the comparative: cheap → cheaper; nice → nicer; pretty → prettier; big → bigger.
>
> ▶ With adjectives of three or more syllables, use *more* + adjective to form the comparative: expensive → more expensive.

A Write the comparatives of these adjectives.

1. attractive ...... *more attractive* ......
2. boring ....
3. exciting ....
4. friendly ....
5. interesting ....
6. reasonable ....
7. sad ....
8. warm ....

B Answer the questions. Use the words in parentheses in your answer. Then write another sentence with the second word.

1. Which pants do you prefer, the cotton ones or the wool ones? (wool / attractive)
   ...... I prefer the wool ones. They're more attractive than the cotton ones ......

2. Which ring do you like better, the gold one or the silver one? (silver / interesting)
   ....

3. Which one do you prefer, the silk jacket or the wool jacket? (silk / pretty)
   ....

4. Which ones do you like more, the black shoes or the purple ones? (purple / exciting)
   ....

Unit 4

1 Simple present questions; short answers (page 23)

> ▶ Use *do* + base form for yes/no questions and short answers with I/you/we/they:
> **Do** I/you/we/they **like** rock? Yes, I/you/we/they **do**. No, I/you/we/they **don't**.
> ▶ Use *does* in yes/no questions and short answers with he/she/it: **Does** he/she **like**
> rock? Yes, he/she **does**. No, he/she **doesn't**.
> ▶ Use *don't* and *doesn't* + base form for negative statements: I **don't like** horror
> movies. He **doesn't like** action movies.
> ▶ Remember: Don't add *–s* to the base form: Does she **like** rock? (NOT: ~~Does she~~
> ~~likes rock?~~)
> ▶ Subject pronouns (*I, you, he, she, it, we, they*) usually come before a verb. Object
> pronouns (*me, you, him, her, it, us, them*) usually come after a verb: He likes **her**, but
> she doesn't like **him**.

A Complete the questions and short answers.

1. A: Do you play (play) a musical instrument?
   B: Yes, I do . I play the guitar.
2. A: .... (like) Taylor Swift?
   B: No, ... Joe doesn't like country music.
3. A: .... (like) talk shows?
   B: Yes, ... Lisa is a big fan of them.
4. A: .... (watch) the news on TV?
   B: Yes, ... Kevin and I watch the news every night.
5. A: .... (like) hip-hop?
   B: No, ... But I love R&B.
6. A: .... (listen to) jazz?
   B: No, ... But my parents listen to a lot of classical music.

B Complete the sentences with object pronouns.

1. We don't listen to hip-hop because we really don't like ....it.... .
2. We love your voice. Please sing for ....
3. These sunglasses are great. Do you like .... ?
4. Who is that man? Do you know .... ?
5. Beth looks great in green. It's a really good color for ....

2 *Would*; verb + *to* + verb (page 26)

> ▶ Don't use a contraction in affirmative short answers with *would*: **Would** you **like to**
> **go to** the game? Yes, I **would**. (NOT: ~~Yes, I'd.~~)

Unscramble the questions and answers to complete the conversation.

A: tonight   to see   would you like   with me   a movie
.... ?

B: I would.   yes,   what   to see   would you like
.... ?

A: the new Halle Berry movie   to see   I'd like
....

B: OK. That's a great idea!

Unit 5

1 Present continuous (page 32)

▶ Use the present continuous to talk about actions that are happening now: What **are** you **doing (these days)**? I**'m studying** English.

▶ The present continuous is present of *be* + *-ing*. For verbs ending in *e*, drop the *e* and add *–ing*: have → having, live → living.

▶ For verbs ending in vowel + consonant, double the consonant and add *–ing*: sit → sitting.

Write questions with the words in parentheses and the present continuous. Then complete the responses with short answers or the verbs in the box.

live	study	take	✓ teach	work

1. A: (what / your sister / do / these days) <u>What's your sister doing these days?</u>
   B: <u>She's teaching</u> English.
   A: Really? (she / live / abroad) ....
   B: Yes, ... She .... in South Korea
2. A: (how / you / spend / your summer) ....
   B: I .... part-time. I .... two classes also.
   A: (what / you / take) ....
   B: My friend and I .... photography and Japanese. We like our classes a lot.

2 Quantifiers (page 34)

▶ Use *a lot of, all, few, nearly all* before plural nouns: **A lot of/All/Few/Nearly all** families are small. Use *no one* before a verb: **No one** gets married before the age of 18.

▶ *Nearly all* means "almost all."

Read the sentences about the small town of Monroe. Rewrite the sentences using the quantifiers in the box. Use each quantifier only once.

a lot of	all	few	nearly all	✓ no one

1. In Monroe, 0% of the people drive before the age of 16.
   <u>In Monroe, no one drives before the age of 16.</u>
2. Ninety-eight percent of students finish high school.
   ....
3. One hundred percent of children start school by the age of six.
   ....
4. Eighty-nine percent of couples have more than one child.
   ....
5. Twenty-three percent of families have more than four children.
   ....

Unit 6

1 Adverbs of frequency (page 37)

> ▶ Adverbs of frequency (*always, almost always, usually, often, sometimes, hardly ever, almost never, never*) usually come before the main verb: She **never plays** tennis. I **almost always eat** breakfast. BUT Adverbs of frequency usually come after the verb *be*: I'**m always** late.
>
> ▶ *Usually* and *sometimes* can begin a sentence: **Usually** I walk to work. **Sometimes** I exercise in the morning.
>
> ▶ Some frequency expressions usually come at the end of a sentence: *every day, once a week, twice a month, three times a year*: Do you exercise **every day**? I exercise **three times a week**.

Put the words in order to make questions. Then complete the answers with the words in parentheses.

1. you   what   weekends   usually   do   do   on
   Q: *What do you usually do on weekends?* ....
   A: I .... (often / play sports)
2. ever   you   go jogging   do   with a friend
   Q: ....
   A: No, ... (always / alone)
3. you   play   do   tennis   how often
   Q: ....
   A: I .... (four times a week)
4. do   you   what   in the evening   usually   do
   Q: ....
   A: My family and I .... (almost always / watch TV)
5. go   how often   you   do   to the gym
   Q: ....
   A: I .... (never)

2 Questions with *how*; short answers (page 40)

> ▶ Don't confuse *good* and *well*. Use the adjective *good* with *be* and the adverb *well* with other verbs: How **good** are you at soccer? BUT How **well** do you play soccer?

Complete the questions with *How* and a word from the box. Then match the questions and the answers.

good   long   often   well

1. .... do you lift weights? ....   a. Not very well, but I love it.
2. .... do you play tennis? ....   b. About six hours a week.
3. .... are you at aerobics? ....   c. Not very often. I prefer aerobics.
4. .... do you spend at the gym? ....   d. Pretty good, but I hate it.

Unit 7

1 Simple past (page 45)

> ► Use *did* with the base form – not the past form – of the main verb in questions: How **did** you **spend** the weekend? (NOT: How did you spent . . .?)
> ► Use *didn't* with the base form in negative statements: We **didn't go** shopping. (NOT: . . . we didn't went shopping.)

Complete the conversation.

A: ....Did.... you ...have.... (have) a good weekend?
B: Yes, I .... I .... (have) a great time. My sister and I .... (go) shopping on Saturday. We .... (spend) all day at the mall.
A: .... you .... (buy) anything special?
B: I .... (buy) a new laptop. And I .... (get) some new clothes, too.
A: Lucky you! What clothes .... you .... (buy)?
B: Well, I .... (need) some new boots. I .... (find) some great ones at Luff's Department Store.
A: What about you? What .... you .... (do) on Saturday?
B: I .... (not do) anything special. I .... (stay) home and .... (work) around the house. Oh, but I .... (see) a really good movie on TV. And then I .... (make) dinner with my mother. I actually .... (enjoy) the day.

2 Past of *be* (page 47)

> | ► Present | | Past |
> |---|---|---|
> | am/is | → | **was** |
> | are | → | **were** |

Rewrite the sentences. Find another way to write each sentence using *was, wasn't, were,* or *weren't* and the words in parentheses.

1. Tony didn't come to class yesterday. (in class)
   Tony wasn't in class yesterday.

2. He worked all day. (at work)
   ....

3. Tony and his co-workers worked on Saturday, too. (at work)
   ....

4. They didn't go to work on Sunday. (at work)
   ....

5. Did Tony stay home on Sunday? (at home)
   ....

6. Where did Tony go on Sunday? (on Sunday)
   ....

7. He and his brother went to a baseball game. (at a baseball game)
   ....

8. They stayed at the park until 7:00. (at the park)
   ....

Unit 8

1 *There is, there are; one, any, some* (page 51)

> ▶ Don't use a contraction in a short answer with *Yes*: Is there a hotel near here? Yes, **there is**. (NOT: ~~Yes, there's.~~)
> ▶ Use *some* in affirmative statements and *any* in negative statements: There are **some** grocery stores in my neighborhood, but there aren't **any** restaurants. Use *any* in most questions: Are there **any** nice stores around here?

Complete the conversations. Circle the correct words.

1. A: **Is / Are** there any supermarkets in this neighborhood?
   B: No, there **isn't / aren't**, but there are **one / some** on Main Street.
   A: And **is / are** there a post office near here?
   B: Yes, **there's / there is**. It's across from the bank.
2. A: **Is / Are** there a gas station around here?
   B: Yes, **there's / there are** one behind the shopping center.
   A: Great! And are there **a / any** coffee shops nearby?
   B: Yes, there's a good **one / some** in the shopping center.

2 Quantifiers; *how many* and *how much* (page 54)

> ▶ Use *a lot* with both count and noncount nouns: Are there many traffic lights on First Avenue? Yes, there are **a lot**. Is there much traffic? Yes, there's **a lot**.
> ▶ Use *any* – not *none* – in negative statements: How much traffic is there on your street? There **isn't any**. = There**'s none**. (NOT: ~~There isn't none.~~)
> ▶ Use *How many* with count nouns: **How many books** do you have?
> ▶ Use *How much* with noncount nouns: **How much traffic** is there?

A Complete the conversations. Circle the correct words.

1. A: Is there **many / much** traffic in your city?
   B: Well, there's **a few / a little**.
2. A: Are there **many / much** public telephones around here?
   B: No, there aren't **many / none**.
3. A: **How many / How much** restaurants are there in your neighborhood?
   B: There **is / are** a lot.
4. A: **How many / How much** noise **is / are** there in your city?
   B: There's **much / none**. It's very quiet.

B Write questions with the words in parentheses. Use *much* or *many*.

1. A: *Is there much pollution in your neighborhood?* .... (pollution)
   B: No, there isn't. My neighborhood is very clean.
2. A: .... (parks)
   B: Yes, there are. They're great for families.
3. A: .... (crime)
   B: There's none. It's a very safe part of the city.
4. A: .... (laundromats)
   B: There aren't any. A lot of people have their own washing machines.

Grammar plus answer key

Unit 1

1 Statements with *be*; possessive adjectives

1. This **is** Delia Rios. **She's** a new student from Peru.
2. My name **is** Sergio. **I'm** from Brazil.
3. My brother and I **are** students here. **Our** names are Dave and Jeff.
4. **He's** Yoshi. **He's** 19 years old.
5. **They're** in my English class. **It's** a very big class.

2 Wh-questions with *be*

1. f
2. e
3. a
4. b
5. c
6. d

3 Yes/No questions and short answers with *be*

1. B: No, **they're not / they aren't**. They're in English 2.
2. A: Hi! **Are you** in this class?
   B: Yes, **I am**. I'm a new student here.
3. A: **Are you** from the United States?
   B: No, **we're not / we aren't**. We're from Montreal, Canada.
4. A: Hi, Sonia. **Are you** free?
   B: No, **I'm not**. I'm on my way to class.
5. A: That's the new student. **Is he** from Puerto Rico?
   B: No, **he's not / he isn't**. he's from Costa Rica.
6. A: **Is she** from Thailand?
   B: Yes, **she is**. She's from Bangkok.

Unit 2

1 Simple present Wh-questions and statements

1. A: I **have** good news! Dani **has** a new job.
   B: How **does** she **like** it?
   A: She **loves** it. The hours are great.
   B: What time **does** she **start**?
   A: She **starts** at nine and **finishes** at five.
2. A: What **do** you **do**?
   B: I'm a teacher.
   A: What **do** you **teach**?
   B: I **teach** Spanish, and English.
   A: Really? My sister **teaches** English, too.

2 Time expressions

B: I love it, but the hours are difficult. I start work **at** 7:30 A.M., and I work **until** 3:30.
A: That's interesting! I work the same hours, but I work **at** night. I start **at** 7:30 **in** the evening and finish **at** 3:30 **in** the morning.
B: Wow! What time do you get up?
A: Well, I get home **at** 4:30 and go to bed **at** 5:30. And I sleep **until** 2:00. But I only work **on** weekends, so it's OK. What about you?
B: Oh, I work **on** Monday, Wednesday, and Friday. And I get up **early** – around 6:00 A.M.

Unit 3

1 Demonstratives; *one, ones*

1. A: Excuse me. How much are **these** shoes?
   B: **They're** $279.
   A: And how much is **that** bag over there?
   B: **It's** only $129.
   A: And are the two gray **ones** $129, too?
   B: No. **Those** are only $119.
   A: Oh! **This** store is really expensive.
2. A: Can I help you?
   B: Yes, please. I really like **those** jeans over there. How much **are they**?
   A: Which **ones**? Do you mean **these**?
   B: No, the black **ones**.
   A: Let me look. Oh, **they're** $35.99.
   B: That's not bad. And how much is **this** sweater here?
   A: **It's** only $9.99.

2 Preferences; comparisons with adjectives

A

2. more boring
3. more exciting
4. friendlier
5. more interesting
6. more reasonable
7. sadder
8. warmer

B

2. I like the silver one (better). It's more interesting.
3. I prefer the silk one. It's prettier.
4. I like the purple ones (more). They're more exciting.

Unit 4

1 Simple present questions; short answers

A

2. A: **Does Joe like** Taylor Swift?
   B: No, **he doesn't**.
3. A: **Does Lisa like** talk shows?
   B: Yes, **she does**.
4. A: **Do you / you and Bob watch** the news on TV?
   B: Yes, **we do**.
5. A: **Do you like** hip-hop?
   B: No, **I don't**.
6. A: **Do your parents listen to** jazz?
   B: No, **they don't**.

B

2. us   3. them   4. him   5. her

2 *Would*; verb + *to* + verb

A: Would you like to see a movie with me tonight?
B: Yes, I would. What would you like to see?
A: I'd like to see the new Halle Berry movie.

Unit 5

1 Present continuous

1. A: **Is she living abroad?**
   B: Yes, **she is**. She**'s living / is living** in South Korea.
2. A: **How are you spending your summer?**
   B: **I'm working** part-time. **I'm taking** two classes also.
   A: **What are you taking?**
   B: My friend and I **are studying** photography and Japanese. We like our classes a lot.

2 Quantifiers

2. Nearly all students finish high school.
3. All children start school by the age of six.
4. A lot of couples have more than one child.
5. Few families have more than four children.

Unit 6

1 Adverbs of frequency

1. A: **I often play sports.**
2. Q: **Do you ever go jogging with a friend?**
   A: No, **I always jog / go jogging alone.**
3. Q: **How often do you play tennis?**
   A: **I play four times a week.**
4. Q: **What do you usually do in the evening?**
   A: My family and I almost always watch TV.
5. Q: **How often do you go to the gym?**
   A: **I never go (to the gym).**

2 Questions with *how*; short answers

1. **How often** do you lift weights? c
2. **How well** do you play tennis? a
3. **How good** are you at aerobics? d
4. **How long** do you spend at the gym? b

Unit 7

1 Simple past

B: Yes, I **did**. I **had** a great time. My sister and I **went** shopping on Saturday. We **spent** all day at the mall.
A: **Did** you **buy** anything special?
B: I **bought** a new laptop. And I **got** some new clothes, too.
A: Lucky you! What clothes **did** you **buy**?
B: Well, I **needed** some new boots. I **found** some great ones at Luff's Department Store.
A: What about you? What **did** you **do** on Saturday?
B: I **didn't do** anything special. I **stayed** home and **worked** around the house. Oh, but I **saw** a really good movie on TV. And then I **made** dinner with my mother. I actually **enjoyed** the day.

2 Past of *be*

2. He was at work all day.
3. Tony and his co-workers were at work on Saturday, too.
4. They weren't at work on Sunday.
5. Was Tony at home on Sunday?
6. Where was Tony on Sunday?
7. He and his brother were at a baseball game.
8. They were at the park until 7:00.

Unit 8

1 *There is, there are; one, any, some*

1. A: **Are** there any supermarkets in this neighborhood?
   B: No, there **aren't**, but there are **some** on Main Street.
   A: And **is** there a post office near here?
   B: Yes, **there is**. It's across from the bank.
2. A: **Is** there a gas station around here?
   B: Yes, **there's** one behind the shopping center.
   A: Great! And are there **any** coffee shops nearby?
   B: Yes, there's a good **one** in the shopping center.

2 Quantifiers; *how many* and *how much*

A

1. A: much
   B: a little
2. A: many
   B: many
3. A: How many
   B: are
4. A: How much
   B: none

B

2. A: Are there many parks?
3. A: Is there much crime?
4. A: Are there many laundromats?

Credits

Illustrations

Andrezzinho: 32, 60, 120; **Ilias Arahovitis:** 17 (*bottom center, right*), 117, 126; **Ralph Butler:** 88, 102; **Mark Collins:** v; **Paul Daviz:** 33, 59, 90 (*top*); **Rob De Bank:** 17 (*center*), 42; **Carlos Diaz:** 127; **Tim Foley:** 17 (*bottom left*); **Travis Foster:** 14, 68, 71; **Chuck Gonzales:** 11, 16 (*bottom*), 37, 100 (*bottom*); **Jim Haynes:** 19, 25 (*bottom*), 93, 106; **Dan Hubig:** 17 (*top*), 18, 40; **Randy Jones:** 9, 39, 44, 85, 86 (*bottom*), 91, 108, 110, 116, 117; **Trevor Keen:** 25 (*top*), 53 (*top*), 58, 100 (*top*); **Joanna Kerr:** 50 (*top*), 80, 121

Kja-artists: 4, 70, 107; **Eric Larsen:** 115; **Shelton Leong:** 2, 3, 5, 129; **Monika Melnychuk:** 20; **Karen Minot:** 16 (*top*), 51, 55, 92; **Rob Schuster:** 28, 36 (*bottom*), 77, 86 (*top*), 100 (*top*), 105, 122, 128; **Daniel Vasconcellos:** 78 (*top*), 113, 131; **Brad Walker:** 50 (*bottom*), 61 (*bottom*), 81; **Sam Whitehead:** 31, 53 (*bottom*), 64 (*bottom*), 66, 67, 78 (*bottom*), 79, 114; **James Yamasaki:** 30, 47, 56, 103, 123, 124; **Rose Zgodzinski:** 36 (*top*), 38, 74, 96, 111, 125; **Carol Zuber-Mallison:** 61(*top*), 69, 83, 89, 97, 118

Photos

6 (*top to bottom*) © Echo/Cultura/Getty Images; © Hemera/Thinkstock
7 © Jill Fromer/iStockphoto
8 (*clockwise from top left*) © Rich Legg/iStockphoto; © Zhang Bo/iStockphoto; © AP Photo/Phil Sandlin; © Jose Luis Pelaez Inc/Blend Images; © Fuse/Getty Images; © Radius Images/Alamy
9 (*left to right*) © Glowimages RM/Alamy; © Rudyanto Wijaya/iStockphoto; © Joe Belanger/Shutterstock; © West Coast Surfer/Moodboard/Age Fotostock; © Jeff Greenberg/Alamy; © Jose Luis Pelaez Inc./Blend Images
10 (*top to bottom*) © Tetra Images/Alamy; © Ariel Skelley/Blend Images
11 © Yellow Dog Productions/Lifesize/Getty Images
12 (*top to bottom*) © Duard van der Westhuizen/Shutterstock; © Purestock/Getty Images
13 (*all*) (Eddie Chen) © Red Chopsticks/Getty Images; (Julia Brown) © Andrew Rich/iStockphoto; (Denise Parker) © Roberto Westbrook/Blend Images/Getty Images
15 (*top, left to right*) © Digital Vision/Thinkstock; © Kent Meireis/The Image Works; © Lothar Wels/Masterfile; © LWA/Dann Tardif/Blend Images/Getty Images; (*bottom*) © iStockphoto/Thinkstock
19 (*top, left to right*) © Terex/Fotolia; © Hemera/Thinkstock; © Hemera Technologies/AbleStock.com/Thinkstock; © largeformat4x5/iStockphoto; (*middle, left to right*) © Gary Alvis/iStockphoto; © Vedius/Alamy; © Stockbyte/Thinkstock; © Terex/iStockphoto
21 (*top right*) © Sean Locke/iStockphoto; (*middle, left*) © Leaf/Veer
23 (*top to bottom*) © Jemal Countess/Getty Images; © m78/ZUMA Press/Newscom; © AP Photo/Paul Drinkwater
24 (*middle, left to right*) © Sthanlee B. Mirador Pacific Rim/Newscom; © Jeffrey R. Staab/CBS Photo Archive/Getty Images; (*bottom, left to right*) © FRANCK FIFE/AFP/Getty Images; © g90/ZUMA Press/Newscom
27 (*top to bottom*) © Paul Gilham/FIFA/Getty Images; © MGM/Courtesy Everett Collection; © Ronald Martinez/Getty Images
28 (*all*) (wool pants) © Gordana Sermek/Shutterstock; (silk shirt) © PhotoObjects.net/Thinkstock; (laptop, desktop, cotton shirt) © iStockphoto/Thinkstock
29 © Robert Holmes/Corbis
31 (*all*) (Chris Martin) © Steve Granitz/WireImage/Getty Images; (Francis Ford Coppola) © Steve Mack/WireImage/Getty Images; (Miley Cyrus) © Steve Granitz/WireImage/Getty Images; (Casey Affleck) © Kurt Krieger/Corbis; (Gwyneth Paltrow) © Steve Granitz/WireImage/Getty Images; (Nicholas Cage) © Pier Giorgio Brunelli/FilmMagic/Getty Images; (Billy Ray Cyrus) © Steve Granitz/WireImage/Getty Images; (Jennifer Garner) © Nancy Kaszerman/ZUMA Press/Corbis
34 (*top to bottom*) © Lane Oatey/Getty Images; © iStockphoto/Thinkstock; © Westend61/SuperStock
35 (*clockwise from left*) © Jose Luis Pelaez Inc/Blend Images; © Juice Images/Cultura/Getty Images; © BananaStock/Thinkstock
37 © Jupiterimages/Brand X Pictures/Thinkstock
38 (*left to right*) © Mango Productions/Comet/Corbis; © Goodshoot/Thinkstock; © Ilja Mašík/Shutterstock; © Tetra Images/Alamy; © Ale Ventura/PhotoAlto/Photolibrary
39 (*left to right*) © Ben Queenborough/BPI/Corbis; © Robert Cianflone/Getty Images
40 © DiMaggio/Kalish/Corbis
43 © Ocean/Corbis
44 (*top, left to right*) © imagebroker/Alamy; © iStockphoto/Thinkstock; © Imagesource/Photolibrary; © Filaphoto/Shutterstock; (*middle, left to right*) © Skip ODonnell/iStockphoto; © Martin Moxter/Photolibrary; © Arctic-Images/Alamy; © James Steidl/iStockphoto
46 © Sean Cayton/The Image Works
47 © Manamana/Shutterstock
48 © iStockphoto/Thinkstock
49 (*top to bottom*) © Tibor Bognár/Age Fotostock; © IanDagnall/Alamy; © blickwinkel/Alamy
52 © Dennis MacDonald/Age Fotostock

54 © Tim Graham/Getty Images
55 © Jean Heguy/First Light/Alamy
60 © Comstock/Thinkstock
61 (*top, left to right*) © Hemera/Thinkstock; © Koki Iino/Getty Images; © Ryan McVay/Stone/Getty Images
63 (*top, right*) © Jupiterimages/Thinkstock; (*middle, top to bottom*) © Stefan Gosatti/Getty Images; © Francois Guillot/AFP/Getty Images; © Rudy k/Alamy
64 (*top, left to right*) © Franz Marc Frei/Look/Age Fotostock; © John Elk III/Alamy; © Jim West/Age Fotostock; © Antonella Carri/Marka/Age Fotostock; © Wendy Kaveney/Danita Delimont/Alamy
69 (*clockwise from top*) © Scholz/Mauritius Images/Age Fotostock; © Andrew Peacock/Getty Images; © Chappuis Blaise/Rapsodia/Age Fotostock
72 (*top to bottom*) © Gerth Roland/Age Fotostock; © Nik Wheeler/Corbis; © Walter Bibikow/Age Fotostock
73 © Mark L Stephenson/Surf/Corbis
74 (*middle*) © John Coletti/JAI/Corbis; (*bottom, clockwise from left*) © Katja Kreder/Imagebroker/Alamy; © Joel Saget/AFP/Getty Images; © R Sigaev/Zoonar/Age Fotostock; © Supri/RTR/Newscom; © Florian Kopp/imagebroker/Age Fotostock; © Hermes Images/Tips Images RM/Age Fotostock
75 © Frilet Patrick/Hemis/Alamy
76 (*top*) © EckPhoto/Alamy; (*bottom*) © Philippe Michel/Age Fotostock/Photolibrary
77 (*top to bottom*) © Timothy Allen/Axiom Photographic Agency/Getty Images; © Greg Johnston/Danita Delimont/Alamy; © Chris Caldicott/Axiom Photographic Agency/Age Fotostock
80 © Brand X Pictures/Thinkstock
81 © Beauty Photo Studio/Age Fotostock
82 © Bill Ling/Digital Vision/Getty Images
83 (*top, right*) © Thornton Cohen/Alamy; (*middle*) © John Glover/Alamy
86 (*top, left to right*) © Esbin-Anderson/Age Fotostock; © Hamza Türkkol/iStockphoto; © iStockphoto/Thinkstock; © Bronze Photography/Healthy Food Images/Age Fotostock; (*middle, left to right*) © Iryna Dobrovyns'ka/iStockphoto; © iStockphoto/Thinkstock; © Dino Osmic/iStockphoto; © ALEAIMAGE/iStockphoto
87 (*middle, clockwise from left*) (healthy, delicious, rich) © iStockphoto/Thinkstock; © Polka Dot/Thinkstock; © Vikif/iStockphoto; © Hemera/Thinkstock; © Digital Vision/Thinkstock
89 © foodfolio/Alamy
90 © Jose Luis Pelaez, Inc./Corbis
94 (*middle, left to right*) © Shelly Perry/iStockphoto; © iStockphoto/Thinkstock; © Photos.com/Thinkstock
95 © Robert Harding/Digital Vision/Getty Images
96 © TongRo Image Stock/Alamy
97 (*top, left to right*) © Comstock/Thinkstock; © Kim Karpeles/Alamy; © iStockphoto/Thinkstock; © Dian Lofton; (*middle, left to right*) © iStockphoto/Thinkstock; © Joy Brown/Shutterstock; © Andre Blais/Shutterstock; © Trista/Shutterstock
99 © Classic Vision/Age Fotostock
102 © Daniel Boczarski/Getty Images
109 (*middle, top to bottom*) © Image Source/Alamy; © Creatas/Thinkstock; © Blend Images/Getty Images
112 © Craig Ferguson/Alamy
118 (*middle, clockwise from left*) © David Lyons/Alamy; © Jeff Greenberg/Age Fotostock; © Valerie Armstrong/Alamy; © Javier Pierini/Stone/Getty Images
119 (*top, left to right*) © DreamPictures/Blend Images; © Jack Hollingsworth/Digital Vision/Thinkstock; © Todd Warnock/Lifesize/Thinkstock
130 (*bottom, left to right*) © David Leahy/Taxi/Getty Images; © Tokyo Feminine Styling/Getty Images; © Masterfile.